LABOUR

LABOUR

Georg Lukács

Translated by David Fernbach

MERLIN PRESS
LONDON

First published in this edition by
The Merlin Press Ltd.,
3 Manchester Road,
London E14

Printed in Great Britain by
Whitstable Litho Ltd.,
Whitstable, Kent

TRANSLATOR'S NOTE

This text forms the first chapter of Part Two of Lukács's work *Toward the Ontology of Social Being*. It is based partly on a manuscript that, though incomplete, was corrected by the author, and partly on Lukács's dictated transcript. Numbered footnotes are Lukács's own, although Lukács's references to German-language works have generally been replaced by references to the standard English translations. Additional footnotes indicated by an asterisk are those inserted by the German editors. A contents list for the *Ontology* as a whole can be found at the end of this volume.

CONTENTS

In seeking to present the specific categories of social being ontologically, how they arise out of earlier forms of being, how they are linked with these, based on them and yet distinct from them, we must begin the attempt with an analysis of labour. It must not be forgotten, of course, that each grade of being has a complex character, as a whole as well as in detail, so that even its most striking and decisive categories can only be adequately conceived starting from the overall character of the level of being in question. And even the most superficial glance at social being shows how indissolubly intertwined are its decisive categories such as labour, speech, cooperation and division of labour, showing new connections between consciousness and reality and therefore of consciousness to itself. None of these can be adequately grasped when considered in isolation; think for example of the fetishization of the technical aspects as 'discovered' by positivism. This had a profound influence on certain Marxists (Bukharin), and plays a not inconsiderable role even today, not only for those who blindly glorify the universality of manipulation, which is so influential at the present time, but also among those who seek to refute this in the dogmatic manner of abstract ethics.

To clear up the confusion over this question, therefore, we must return to Marx's own dual method which we have already analysed, first breaking down the new complex of being by the way of analytic abstraction, as a prelude to returning (or advancing) on the foundation thus obtained towards the complex of social being not simply as something just given and hence merely envisaged pictorially, but as something comprehended in its real totality. In this connection, the developmental tendencies of the various types of being which we have already investigated in a similar manner give us a definite methodological support. Present-day science is beginning to track down in a concrete way the genesis of

i

the organic from the inorganic, by showing how in certain specific conditions (atmosphere, air pressure, etc.) certain extremely primitive complexes can emerge which already bear within them the fundamental characteristics of the organic, in embryonic form. Naturally, these can no longer exist in the concrete conditions of today, and can only be demonstrated by producing them experimentally. The doctrine of biological evolution then shows us how the specific categories of organic reproduction gradually gain the upper hand in these organisms, in a very contradictory way, and with many blind alleys. It is characteristic, for example, that plants complete their entire reproduction—as a general rule, the exceptions here being unimportant—on the basis of a metabolism with inorganic nature. Only in the animal kingdom does this metabolism come to be conducted purely or at least predominantly in the organic realm, so that—as a general rule, again—even the inorganic substances needed are first worked up by a mediation of this kind. The path of evolution leads to the maximum dominance of the specific categories of a sphere of life over those that derive their existence and efficacy in an insuperable way from the lower sphere of being.

As for social being, it is the organic that plays this role (and of course also the inorganic world through its mediation). In a different context we have already depicted a developmental direction of this kind in the social sphere, what Marx called the 'retreat of the natural boundary'. In this connection, of course, experimental evidence of transitions from the predominantly organic to the predominantly social are ruled out from the start. The social here and now of such a transition stage cannot be reconstructed experimentally, precisely because of the radical irreversibility of social being. Thus we cannot gain any immediate and precise knowledge of this transformation from organic being into social. The most we can reach is a *post festum* knowledge, by application of the

Marxist method. As the human anatomy provides the key to the anatomy of the ape, so the more primitive stage can be reconstructed in thought from the higher stage, from its developmental tendencies and direction. Archaeological excavations, perhaps, give us the greatest degree of approximation, by casting light on various steps of a transition that is not only anatomical and physiological, but also social (tools, etc.). Yet the leap remains a leap, and in the last analysis it can only be made clear by intellectual comprehension, through the thought experiment indicated.

We must always be quite clear, therefore, that what is involved here is an ontologically necessary transition, by such a leap, from one level of being to another which is qualitatively different. The hope held by the first generation of Darwinians of finding the 'missing link' between man and animal was bound to prove vain, since biological characteristics can only illuminate the transition stages, and never the leap itself. We have also pointed out, however, that descriptions of the psycho-physical distinctions between man and animal, be they ever so precise, must still pass over the ontological fact of this leap (and the real process in which it is effected), as long as they cannot explain the rise of these human properties in terms of human social life. Just as little can the essence of these new connections be explained by psychological experiments with higher animals, e.g., apes. In experiments of this kind, the artificiality induced into the living conditions of these animals is easily forgotten. Firstly, the insecurity of their natural existence is removed (the search for food, the dangers to which they are subject), while secondly, the tools which they work with are not self-made, but produced and selected by the experimenter. The essence of human labour, however, depends firstly on its arising amid the struggle for existence, and secondly on all steps of its development being products of man's own self-activity. Certain similarities, therefore, which are often strongly over-emphasized, must in fact be treated extremely critically. The only aspect here which is genuinely instructive is the great elasticity displayed by the higher animals' behaviour; the species in which the leap to labour was actually achieved must have been a special border case, still more developed in quality. In this respect, however, those species that exist today are evidently at a far lower level, and cannot bridge the gap towards genuine labour.

Since what is involved here is the concrete complex of the social as a form of being, it is justifiable to raise the question as to why it is particularly labour that we extract from this complex and ascribe this preferred position in the process, for the genetic leap. When viewed ontologically, the answer is more simple than it might appear at first sight. It is because all other categories of this form of being are already by nature purely social in character; their properties and modes of efficacy develop only in a social being that is already constituted, and however primitive may be the manner of their appearance, they thus presuppose the leap to have already been achieved. Only with labour does its ontological nature give it a pronounced transition character. It is by its very nature a relationship of interchange between man (society) and nature, and moreover with inorganic nature (tool, raw material, object of labour) as well as organic, and although this relationship can also figure at certain points in the series just indicated, it characterizes above all the transition in the working man himself from purely biological being to social being. Marx, therefore, was quite right to say:

'Labour, then, as the creator of use-values, as useful labour, is a condition of human existence which is independent of all forms of society; it is an eternal natural necessity which mediates the metabolism between man and nature, and therefore human life itself.'[1]

Even in our present consideration of the genetic process, it would be wrong to object to the expression 'use-value', as

iv

far too economic a term at this stage. For before use-value becomes bound up with exchange-value in a relationship of reflection, which can only happen at a relatively far higher stage, use-value means nothing more than a product of labour which man is able to make use of in the reproduction of his existence. All those determinations which we shall see to make up the essence of what is new in social being, are contained *in nuce* in labour. Thus labour can be viewed as the original phenomenon, as the model for social being, and the elucidation of these determinations already gives so clear a picture of the essential features of social being that it seems methodologically advantageous to begin by analysing labour.

Yet we must always be clear in this connection that it is an abstraction to consider labour, as assumed here, in this isolated way. Even if social life, the first division of labour, language, etc., arise from labour, they do so not in any temporal sequence that can be simply ascertained, but in an essentially simultaneous manner. The abstraction we are making here is thus an abstraction *sui generis;* from the methodological standpoint it has a similar character to those abstractions that we dealt with in detail in analysing the intellectual construction of Marx's *Capital.* We shall only be able to abandon this abstraction in the next chapter, when we come to investigate the reproduction process of social being. This form of abstraction, therefore, for us as for Marx, does not mean that problems of this kind can be completely made to disappear—even if only temporarily—but simply that they are as it were put on one side, appearing only on the horizon while their proper, concrete and all-round investigation is held over for later stages of analysis. For the time being, they come to the fore only in as much as they are directly connected with labour, itself abstractly conceived, being its direct ontological consequences.

1. Labour as a Teleological Positing

It is to Engels we are indebted for having ascribed labour the central role in man's coming to be human. Engels, too, investigates the biological precondition of its new role in this leap from animal to man. He finds it in the differentiation made of the function of the hand, present already with the apes.

'The hands are used mainly for gathering and holding food in the same way as the fore paws of the lower mammals are used. Many apes use their hands to build themselves nests in the trees, or even to construct roofs between the branches to protect themselves against the weather, as the chimpanzee, for example, does. With their hands they grasp sticks to defend themselves against enemies, and with their hands they bombard their enemies with fruits and stones.'[1]

But Engels is equally at pains to point out that despite anticipations of this kind, there is a leap involved here, no longer belonging simply to the organic sphere, but signifying a qualitative and ontological advance of principle beyond this. It is with this in mind that Engels says, comparing the hands of the ape and of man:

'The number and general arrangement of the bones and muscles are the same in both hands, but the hand of the lowest savage can perform hundreds of operations that no simian hand can imitate—no simian hand has ever fashioned even the crudest stone knife.'

1

In this connection Engels stresses the extremely protracted process involved in this transition, which however does not alter its character as a leap. A careful and correct approach to ontological problems always requires one to keep constantly in mind that every leap signifies a qualitative and structural change in being, in the course of which, though the transition stage may contain certain preconditions and possibilities of the later, higher stage, the latter cannot be developed from the former in a simple straight-line continuity. What gives the leap its characteristic nature is this break with the normal continuity of development, and not whether the rise of the new form of being is sudden rather than gradual. As far as concerns the key question of the nature of this leap in the case of labour, we shall come on to this in a moment. First we must just mention how Engels is quite correct here in deriving social life and language directly from labour. These are questions that we shall only be able to deal with later, according to the programme we have laid down. But one aspect should just be briefly noted here, i.e., that so-called animal societies (just as every 'division of labour' in the animal world) are biologically fixed differentiations, as can best be observed in the 'state' of the bees. Irrespective therefore of how an organization of this kind might have arisen, it does not in itself possess any immanent potential for further development, being no more than a particular mode of adaptation of an animal species to its environment. The more perfectly this 'division of labour' functions, and the more firmly it is biologically rooted, the less its future potential. But the division of labour created by labour in human society, on the contrary, produces, as we shall see, its own conditions of reproduction, and in such a way, moreover, that simple reproduction of the hitherto existing conditions is simply the border case of what is more typically expanded reproduction. This does not of course rule out the presence of blind alleys in development; but their causes are always determined by the structure of the society of the time, and not by the biological properties of its members.

Marx had the following to say on the nature of labour that has already become adequate:

'We presuppose labour in a form in which it is an exclusively human characteristic. A spider conducts operations which resemble those of the weaver, and a bee would put many a human architect to shame by the construction of its honey-comb cells. But what distinguishes the worst architect from the best of bees is that the architect builds the cell in his mind before he constructs it in wax. At the end of every labour process, a result emerges which had already been conceived by the worker at the beginning, hence already existed ideally. Man not only effects a change of form in the materials of nature; he also realizes his own purpose in those materials. And this is a purpose he is conscious of, it determines the mode of his activity with the rigidity of a law, and he must subordinate his will to it.'[2]

This spells out labour's key ontological category. Through labour, a teleological positing is realized within material being, as the rise of a new objectivity. The first consequence of this is that labour becomes the model for any social practice, for in such social practice—no matter how ramified its mediations—teleological positings are always realized, and ultimately realized materially. Certainly, as we shall go on to see, this model character that labour has for the actions of man in society should not be overstretched in a schematic way; yet it is precisely consideration of the most important distinctions that shows the essential ontological affinity, for these very distinctions reveal how labour can serve us in understanding other social-teleological positings because it is their original form as far as being is concerned. The simple fact that labour is the realization of a teleological positing is for anyone an elementary experience of everyday life, and it is therefore an indelible component of any kind of thinking, from everyday conversation through to economy and philosophy. The problem that arises here, therefore, is not for or against labour's teleological character; the only problem, rather, is to subject the almost unlimited generalization of this elementary fact—again from everyday life through to myth, religion and philosophy—to a genuinely critical ontological treatment.

It is in no way surprising, therefore, that those major thinkers who have been strongly oriented towards social existence, such as Aristotle and Hegel, have been clearest in grasping the teleological character of labour, and that their structural analyses only require a few additions, and some corrections that are in no way fundamental, to maintain their validity even today. The real ontological problem arises from the way that the teleological positing is not confined to labour (or in the expanded but justifiable sense to human practice in general), but is rather erected into a general cosmological category, thus giving rise to a persistent relationship of competition, an irresolvable antinomy between causality and teleology such as has marked the entire history of philosophy. And this is done even by Aristotle and Hegel. It is well known how the charming operation of purposiveness in Aristotle's organic—and concern with biology and medicine left a deep and lasting influence on his thought—is fascinating for the way that his system ascribes a decisive role to an objective teleology of reality. Similarly well known is the way that Hegel, who depicted the teleological character of labour still more concretely and dialectically than Aristotle, made teleology into the motor of history and hence of his total world view. (We have already indicated some of these problems in the chapter on Hegel.) Thus this antithesis pervades the entire history of thought and the religions, from the beginnings of philosophy through to Leibniz's pre-established harmony.

If we refer to the religions here, this is based in the

property of teleology as an objective ontological category. In other words, while causality is a principle of motion on its own basis, maintaining this character even if a causal series has its point of departure in an act of consciousness, teleology is by its very nature a posited category. Every teleological process involves the positing of a goal, and therefore a goal-positing consciousness. To posit, therefore, in this connection, does not mean simply to raise into consciousness, as with other categories, and with causality in particular; with this act of positing, consciousness initiates a real process, precisely a teleological one. The teleological conception of nature and history, therefore, does not just refer to a purpose, an orientation to a goal, but implies that this existence and movement must have a conscious creator both in the overall process and in its details. The need that gives rise to such conceptions of the world, not only with the narrow-minded authors of theodicies in the eighteenth century, but even in such careful and profound thinkers as Aristotle and Hegel, is a basic and primitive human one: the need to make sense of existence, from the course of the world down to the experiences of individual life—indeed, these most of all. Even after the development of the sciences demolished that religious ontology in which the teleological principle could rule the cosmos unrestrained, this primitive and elementary need survived in the thought and feeling of everyday life. What we have in mind here is not just something like the atheist Niels Lyhne, attempting at the deathbed of his child to influence by prayer the teleological course of events directed by God; this is always a fundamental motive force of everyday mental life. Nikolai Hartmann summed up the position very well in his analysis of teleological thought:

'There is the tendency to take every occasion to ask the "reason" why things have to happen in just such a way. "Why does this have to happen to me?" Or: "Why do I have to suffer like this?" "Why did he have to die so young?"

Every event that "affects" us in some way or other suggests a question of this kind, even if it is just the expression of perplexity or helplessness. We silently assume that there must be some good reason; we seek to find a meaning and justification. As if things were so ordained that everything that happens must have a meaning.'

Hartmann also shows how in language, and in the surface expression of thought, the question 'why?' can often be asked with no explicit reference to purpose, yet without in any way rejecting the essential tenet of a final purpose.[3] It is easy to understand how, given the deep roots of this kind of thinking and feeling in everyday life, a radical break with the dominance of teleology in nature, life, etc., is seldom achieved. This residual religious need, so persistently effective in the everyday sphere, also has a spontaneous tendency to rub off rather strongly on areas further afield than immediate personal life.

This conflict is clearly visible in Kant's case. By defining organic life as 'purposiveness without purpose', he hit on a genial way to describe the ontological essence of the organic sphere. His correct criticism demolished the superficial teleology of the theodicists who preceded him, and who saw the realization of a transcendent teleology even in the mere usefulness of one thing for another. He thereby opened the way to a correct knowledge of this sphere of being, since it now appeared possible for connections whose necessity was merely causal (and thus also accidental) to give rise to structures of being whose inner movement (adaptation, reproduction of both individual and species) brought regularities into play that could rightly be described as having an objective purpose for the complexes in question. Yet Kant blocked his own line of advance from these positions to the real problem. Already at the level of methodology, he sought as always to solve ontological questions by epistemology. And since his theory of objectively valid knowledge is exclusively oriented to mathematics and physics, he was necessarily led to the conclusion that his own genial insight could not have any results for scientific knowledge of the organic world. Thus he says in one formulation that has become particularly celebrated: 'It would be absurd for men even to conceive of the idea, or to hope, that some day a future Newton might come along and make intelligible the production of just one single blade of grass, by natural laws with no kind of intention behind them.'[4] The questionable character of this statement lies not only in its refutation by the science of evolution less than a century later, already in the first Darwinian formulation. Engels wrote to Marx after reading Darwin: 'In one aspect, teleology had not yet been killed off, but this has now been done.' And Marx, even though he had reservations about Darwin's method, held that Darwin's work 'contains the natural-historical basis for our own view'.[5]

A further and still more important consequence of Kant's attempt to pose and answer ontological questions epistemologically, is that the ontological problem itself remains ultimately undecided, and that at a 'critically' determined limit of its range, thought is brought to a halt without being able to answer the question positively or negatively. A door for transcendental speculation is left open by epistemological criticism itself, a door for ultimate recognition of the possibility of teleological solutions, even if Kant does not recognize these in the realm of science. What we have in mind here is particularly the conception of the intuitive 'intellectus archetypus', later of decisive importance for Schelling, which we humans do not possess, but whose existence Kant himself saw as 'containing no contradictions',[6] and which is supposedly in a position to resolve these questions. The problem of causality and teleology thus appears equally in the form of the unknowable (for us) thing-in-itself. No matter how often Kant rejects the claims of theology, this rejection is limited to 'our' knowledge, for theology, too, raises the claim to be scientific, and to this extent therefore remains subject to the authority of epistemological criticism. What the issue boils down to here is that in the knowledge of nature causal and teleological modes of explanation are mutually exclusive, but when Kant is analysing human practice, he directs his attention exclusively to its highest, most subtle and most socially derived form, pure morality, which thus does not emerge for him dialectically from the activities of life (society), but stands rather in an essential and insuperable antithesis to these activities. Here again, therefore, the real ontological problem remains unanswered.

As in every genuine question of ontology, here too the correct answer has a character that seems trivial in its immediate appearance, but is steadily at work like a kind of Columbus's egg. We need only consider somewhat more closely the determinations involved in the Marxian solution of labour teleology, however, to see the power these contain, with decisive consequences that unravel far-reaching groups of false problems. It is clear from Marx's attitude towards Darwin, and self-evident for anyone familiar with his thought, that Marx denied the existence of any kind of teleology outside of labour (human practice). Thus Marx's understanding of labour teleology already goes far beyond the attempted solutions of even such great predecessors as Aristotle and Hegel, since for Marx labour is not one of the many phenomenal forms of teleology in general, but rather the only point at which a teleological positing can be ontologically established as a real moment of material actuality. This correct knowledge of reality elucidates a whole series of questions ontologically. First of all, the decisive real characteristic of teleology, that it can attain actuality only as a positing, receives a simple, self-evident and real foundation. We do not have to repeat the definition Marx gave to see that all labour would be impossible if it were not preceded by a positing of

8

this kind, one that determined its process at every step. Certainly, Aristotle and Hegel clearly grasped this essential character of labour; but because they also sought to comprehend the organic world and the course of history in a similarly teleological way, they had always to indicate a subject for this necessary teleological positing (the *Weltgeist* in Hegel's case), which forcibly transformed the reality into a myth. Marx's precise and strictly defined restriction of teleology to labour (to social practice), with teleology being ruled out in all other modes of being, does not cause it to lose its importance; on the contrary, this increases, by our understanding that it is only the highest level of being known to us, social being, that is constitutionally endowed with such a real and effective teleology, as its characteristic feature, raising itself up from the level on which its existence is based, that of organic life, into a new autonomous form of being. We can only reasonably speak of social being when we understand that its genesis, its elevation from its basis and its acquisition of autonomy, is based on labour, i.e., on the ongoing realization of teleological positings.

This initial aspect, however, has very far-reaching philosophical consequences. We know from the history of philosophy the intellectual struggles between causality and teleology as categorical foundations of reality and its movements. Every philosophy with a theological orientation needed to proclaim the superiority of teleology over causality in order to bring its god into mental agreement with the cosmos and the world of man. Even if god simply winds up the world clock to set the system of causality in motion, this hierarchy of creater and creation is unavoidable, and with it the associated priority of the teleological positing. Every pre-Marxist materialism, on the other hand, denying the transcendent creation of the world, had also to challenge the possibility of a really effective teleology. We have just seen how even Kant had to speak—of course in his epistemo-

9

logically-oriented terminology—of the incompatibility of causality and teleology. But once teleology is recognized, as by Marx, as a really effective category, exclusive to labour, the concrete real and necessary coexistence of causality and teleology inexorably follows. These may well remain antitheses, but only within a unitary real process, whose movement is based on the interaction of these antitheses, a process which in order to produce this interaction as a reality, transforms causality, without otherwise violating its nature, into something equally posited.

In order to make this quite clear, we can bring in the analyses of labour by Aristotle and Hegel. Aristotle distinguishes in labour the components of thinking (νόησις) and production (ποίησις). The former serves to posit the goal and to investigate the means of its realization, while the latter serves to attain the realization of the goal thus posited.[7] Now when Hartmann breaks down the former component analytically into two acts, i.e., the positing of the goal and the investigation of the means, he makes concrete in a correct and instructive manner the path-breaking character of Aristotle's idea, while altering no decisive aspect of its ontological nature.[8] For this lies in a mental plan achieving material realization, in the positing of a desired goal bringing about a change in material reality, introducing a material change in reality which represents something qualitatively and radically new in relation to nature. Aristotle's example of the building of a house shows this very concretely. The house is just as material an existence as the stone, wood, etc., of which it is constructed. Yet the teleological positing gives rise to an objectivity which is completely different from that of its elements. The house, of course, cannot be 'derived' from the mere being-in-itself of the stone or wood, not from any kind of further development of their properties, the regularities and powers effective in them. What is necessary for the house is the power of human thought and will, to arrange these

10

properties materially and actually in an essentially quite new connection. Aristotle was in this sense the first to have acknowledged the essential character of this objectivity, which is quite inconceivable in terms of the 'logic' of nature. (Already here, we can see how all the idealist or religious forms of natural teleology, of nature as God's creation, are metaphysical projections of this real model. In the Old Testament story of creation this model is so readily apparent that God not only constantly checks the work he has done—just like the human subject of labour—but also, like a working man, enjoys a rest after finishing his labour. In other creation myths, even if they have directly been given a philosophical form, it is equally easy to recognize the earthly, human labour model; we could mention again the world clock which God has wound up.)

The value of this differentiation made by Hartmann should not be underestimated. Separation of the two acts, the positing of the goal and the investigation of the means, is of the highest importance for an understanding of the labour process, and particularly for its significance in the ontology of social being. Precisely here, we can see the inseparable connection of two categories that are in themselves antithetical, and which viewed abstractly are mutually exclusive; causality and teleology. Investigation of the means of realizing the posited goal must involve an objective knowledge of how to bring about those objectivities and processes which have to be set in motion in order to realize this goal. The positing of the goal and investigation of the means cannot bring anything new into being, in as much as the natural reality as such must remain what it inherently is, a system of complexes whose law-like character persists in complete indifference to all human efforts and ideas. Investigation, in this connection, has a double function. On the one hand it uncovers what is going on independent of any consciousness in the objects in question, while on the other hand it discovers

11

in them new combinations and new functional possibilities which need to be set in motion in order to realize the teleologically posited goal. The being-in-itself of the stone involves no kind of intention, not even an indication that it might be used as a knife or an axe; yet it can only take on this function as a tool if its objectively present properties, as they exist in themselves, are susceptible of a combination which makes this possible. The ontology of this can be seen already at the most primitive level. If primitive man selects a stone with the idea of using it, for example, as an axe, then he must recognize correctly this connection between the properties of the stone—which in many respects have arisen accidentally— and its concrete usability here and now. Only in this way will he have made the act of recognition analysed by Aristotle and Hartmann; and the more developed labour becomes, the clearer is this state of affairs. Hegel, who, as we know, caused a lot of confusion by unduly extending the concept of teleology, correctly recognized this specific nature of labour early on in his work. He wrote in his Jena lectures of 1805-6 that 'nature's own activity, the elasticity of a watch-spring, water, wind, etc., are employed to do things that they would not have done if left to themselves, so that their blind action is made purposive, the opposite of itself'. Man 'allows nature to act on itself, simply looks on and controls it with a light touch'.[9] It is worthy of note that the concept of the cunning of reason, later so important in Hegel's philosophy of history, emerges here in his analysis of labour, probably for the first time. Hegel correctly sees the double-sidedness of this process, on the one hand that the teleological positing 'simply' makes use of nature's own activity, while on the other hand seeing how the transformation of this activity makes it into its own opposite. This natural activity is thus transformed, without a change in the natural ontology of its foundations, into something posited. Hegel thereby describes an ontologically decisive aspect of the role of natural causality in the labour process. Without being subjected to an internal change, the natural objects and natural forces give rise to something completely different; man in his labour can fit their properties, and the laws of their motion, into completely new combinations, endowing them with completely new functions and modes of operation. But since this can only be done from amid the insuperable ontological character of natural laws, the only alteration in the natural categories can consist in the fact that they are posited—in the ontological sense; their positedness is the mediation of their subordination to the determining teleological positing, which is also what makes the posited interweaving of causality and teleology into a unitary and homogenous object, process, etc.

Nature and labour, means and end, thus produce something that is in itself homogenous: the labour process, and finally the product of labour. But the removal of heterogeneities by the unitary character and homogeneity of the positing still has clearly defined limits. We are not referring here at all to the self-evident way that this homogenization presupposes a correct knowledge of causal connections that are not homogenous in reality. If this is missing in the investigation process, these connections cannot be posited at all in the ontological sense. They remain in operation in their natural manner, and the teleological positing is rendered null and void, being reduced, if it is not to be realized, to a necessarily impotent fact of consciousness. Here the distinction between positing in the ontological sense and in that of epistemology can be palpably grasped. Epistemologically, a positing that misses its object is still a positing, even if it must be judged to be false, or possibly incomplete. The ontological positing of causality in the complex of a teleological positing, however, must correctly come to grips with its object, or else it is no positing at all, in this sense. Yet if this contention is not to be exaggerated to the point of untruth, it requires a dialectical qualification. Since any natural object or process presents an intensive infinity of properties, relations of interaction with its environment, etc., what has just been said bears only on those aspects of the intensive infinity that are of positive or negative significance for the teleological positing. Even if all that were necessary for labour was an approximate knowledge of this intensive infinity, as necessarily of this kind, it could never arise at primitive levels of observation of nature (not to speak of knowledge in the conscious sense). This state of affairs should be borne in mind not only because it contains the objective possibility of a boundless higher development of labour, but also because it clearly follows from it that a correct positing, a positing that adequately grasps the causal elements required for the purpose of the moment, in so far as this is concretely needed for the concrete positing of a goal, still remains to be successfully realized in cases when the general ideas about objects, connections, processes, etc., in nature are still completely inadequate in relation to nature as a whole. This dialectic between strict correctness in the more limited area of the concrete teleological positing and a possible and very profound incorrectness in grasping nature in its full being-in-itself, is of very far-reaching importance for the sphere of labour, and we shall deal with this in more detail later on.

The homogenization of end and means as set out above, however, must also be dialectically qualified from another standpoint, and thereby made more concrete. The doubly social character of the positing of the goal—arising as it does from a social need and being called on to satisfy such a need, whereas the naturalness of the substratum of means of realization leads practice directly into a different kind of environment and activity—sets up a fundamental heterogeneity between end and means. The removal of this heterogeneity by its homogenization in the act of positing conceals, as we have just seen, something important and problematic, indicating that the simple subordination of the means to the end is not so simple as it seems at the first immediate glance. We should not in other words lose sight of the straightforward fact that the realizability or otherwise of the posited end depends simply on how far investigation of the means manages to transform natural causality into a posited causality in the ontological sense. The positing of the goal arises from a human social need; yet in order to be a genuine positing of a goal, investigation of the means, i.e., knowledge of nature, must have reached a certain appropriate level; if it has not, then the positing of this goal remains merely a utopian project, a kind of dream, as did flying, for example, from Icarus through to Leonardo and far beyond him. Thus the point at which labour connects with the rise of scientific thought and its development from the standpoint of the ontology of social being is precisely the region described as the investigation of the means. We have already indicated the principle of the new, which even the most primitive labour teleology contains. Now we can add that the continuous production of the new, which is how what we could call the regional category* of the social appears in labour, its first clear elevation from any mere nature-boundedness, is contained in this mode of labour's rise and development. This has the result that the end commands and governs the means in every concrete individual labour process. Yet in speaking of labour processes in their historical continuity and development within the real complexes of social being, we see the rise of a certain reversal of this hierarchical relationship—certainly not an absolute and total reversal, but one that is for all that of the utmost importance for the development of society and humankind. For since the investigation of nature that is indispensable for labour is concentrated above all on the elaboration of means, these means are the principal vehicle of social guarantee that the results of the labour processes are established, the experience of labour continued and particularly further developed. Hence this more adequate knowledge that is the basis of the means (tools, etc.) is often more important for social being itself than is the present satisfaction of the need (the posited end). Hegel recognized this relationship very well. As he put it in his *Logic:*

'But the *means* is the external middle term of the syllogism which is the realization of the end; in the means, therefore, the externality in it manifests itself as such by maintaining itself in the *external other,* and precisely *through* this externality. To this extent the *means* is *superior* to the *finite* ends of *external* purposiveness: the *plough* is more honourable than are immediately the enjoyments procured by it and which are ends. The *tool* lasts, while the immediate enjoyments pass away and are forgotten. By his tools man possesses power over external nature, even though in respects of his ends he is, on the contrary, subject to it.'[10]

We have already followed this train of thought in the chapter on Hegel; yet it does not seem superfluous to repeat it here, since certain very important elements of this relationship are clearly expressed in it. Firstly, Hegel stresses, and by and large rightly so, the longer duration of the means vis-à-vis the immediate ends and fulfilments. To be sure, this antithesis is far from being as sharp in reality as Hegel presents it. For although individual 'immediate enjoyments' certainly do 'pass away' and are forgotten, the satisfaction of needs also has a persistence and continuity when society as a whole is considered. If we recall the reciprocal relationship of production and consumption depicted in the chapter on Marx, we can see how the latter not only maintains and reproduces the former, but also exerts a certain influence on it in its turn. Of course, as we saw there, production is the predominant moment in that relationship (here: the means in the teleological positing), but in Hegel's counterposing of the two, something of its real social significance is passed over as a result of too sharp a confrontation. Secondly, and again correctly, he stresses in connection with the means the aspect of domination 'over external nature', and also with the correct dialectical qualification that man still remains subject to external nature in his positing of ends. Here Hegel's presentation needs to be made more concrete, in as much as while this subjection relates directly to nature—as we have already shown, man can only really posit those goals for which he commands the means of practical realization—what is ultimately involved here is really a social development, the complex which Marx describes as a metabolism between man, i.e., society, and nature, in which connection the social aspect must* unquestionably be the dominant one. In this way the superiority of the means is stressed still more sharply than by Hegel himself. And thirdly, as a result of this situation, the means, the tool, is the most important key for knowledge of those steps of human development for which we do not possess any other evidence. As always, this problem of knowledge conceals an ontological problem. We can often shed light on a period that was completely hidden from view from tools and archaeological excavations alone, as the sole evidence, and can find out much more about the concrete life of the men who used these tools than they seem at first sight to contain. The reason for this is that the tool, when correctly analysed, can yield not only the story of its own creation, but can also open broad perspectives on the mode of life of its users, and even on their conception of the world, etc. We shall be dealing with problems of this kind later on; here we simply want to indicate the extremely general social question of the retreat of the natural boundary, as Gordon Childe describes it so precisely in his analysis of pottery in the period he refers to as the neolithic revolution. His argument hinges above all round the key point of a fundamental distinction between the labour process in pottery and that in the production of tools from stone or bone. 'In making a tool of stone or bone he was always limited by the shape and size of the original material; he could only take bits away from it. No such limitations restrict the activity of the potter. She can form her lump as she wishes; she can go on adding to it without any doubts as to the solidity of the joins.' This makes clear an important point of distinction between two epochs, and indicates the direction in which man liberates himself from the natural material originally used and endows his objects of use with the precise properties required by his social needs. Childe also sees how this process of the retreat of the natural boundary is a gradual one. If the new form is no longer tied to the material found already in existence, it has still arisen from similar assumptions. 'So the earliest pots are obvious imitations of familiar vessels made from other materials—from gourds, from bladders, membranes, and skins, from basketry and wicker-work, or even from human skulls.'[11]

Fourthly, it must still be stressed that investigation of the objects and processes of nature that precedes the positing of causality in the creation of the means, consists in essence of real acts of knowledge and thus objectively contains the beginning, the genesis, of science, even if for a long time this is not consciously recognized. Here, too, we can apply Marx's insight that 'They do not know it, but they do it.' Later in this chapter, we shall deal with the very far-reaching consequences of the connections that thus arise. Here, for the time being, we can only point out that every experience and application of causal connections, i.e., every positing of a real causality, while in labour it figures always as the means for a particular end, has objectively the property of being applicable to something else that may be completely heterogenous. Awareness of this may remain for a long while purely practical, yet in actual fact every successful application to a new area involves correct abstractions which in their objective internal structure already possess important hall-marks of scientific thought. Even though the history of

18

science seldom poses this problem explicitly, it has shown how in many cases extremely abstract and general laws have arisen from the investigation of practical needs and the best method to satisfy them, i.e., from the discovery of the best means in labour. But even apart from this, history shows many examples of how acquisitions of labour, when further abstracted—and we are precisely pointing out that this kind of generalization necessarily arises in the labour process—can grow into the basis of what is already a purely scientific treatment of nature. The genesis of geometry in this way, for example, is a matter of general knowledge. It is not the place here to go into this complex of questions in greater detail, and it must suffice to refer to one interesting case adduced by Bernal, basing himself on Needham's specialist studies of ancient Chinese astronomy. Bernal says that an accurate conception of the circular movement of the night sky around the pole only became possible after the discovery of the wheel. It seems that this idea of rotation was the starting-point of Chinese astronomy. Up to that point, the heavenly world was treated as similar to our own.[12] Thus the inherent tendency for the investigation of means connected with the preparation and execution of the labour process to become autonomous gives rise to scientifically-oriented thinking and later to the various natural sciences. It is not of course just a question of one single genesis of a new area of activity; the genesis is repeated, if in extremely varied forms, in the whole history of the sciences up till today. The model representations that underlie various cosmological and physical hypotheses, etc., are closely connected with, and co-determined by, the ontological conceptions of everyday life at the time, generally unconsciously so, as these in turn are connected with the prevailing experiences, methods and results of labour. Several major turning-points in the sciences have their roots in every-day images of the world owing to labour, which have arisen only gradually, but which at a certain level appear as radically and qualitatively new. The situation prevailing today, when sciences that are already differentiated and to a large extent organized perform preparatory work for industry, while it conceals the basic state of affairs for many people, does not change its actuality in any fundamental ontological respect; it would in fact be interesting to deal more closely from the standpoint of ontological criticism with the influences of this preparatory mechanism on science.

The description of labour given so far, though it is far from complete, already shows how with labour, in comparison with the preceding forms of being, the inorganic and organic, we have a qualitatively new category in the ontology of social being. One such novelty is the realization of the teleological positing as an adequate, considered and willed result. In nature there are only actualities, and an uninterrupted change in their existing concrete forms, an ever-present being other. It is precisely the Marxian theory of labour as the sole existing form of a teleologically produced existence that founds for the first time the specificity of social being. For if the various idealist or religious theories of a general dominance of teleology were to prove correct, the logical conclusion would be that this distinction did not exist at all. Every stone and every fly would be a similar realization of 'labour', the labour of God, or the *Weltgeist,* just like the above described realizations in the teleological positings of human beings. The logical consequence of this could only be that the decisive ontological distinction between society and nature would vanish. Yet when idealist philosophers incline towards dualism, they are particularly concerned to contrast the (apparently) purely spiritual functions of human consciousness, (apparently) completely freed from material reality, with the world of mere material being. No wonder, then, that the terrain of man's own proper activity, his metabolism with nature, which is his starting-point and which he increasingly masters by his practice, above all by his labour, always comes off badly, and that the only human activity that is conceived as genuinely human falls ontologically ready-made from heaven, being presented as a 'timeless' realm of the 'ought', in antithesis to being. (We shall come on shortly to the real genesis of the 'ought' in labour technology.) The contradictions between this conception and the ontological results of modern science are so blatant that they do not need to be dealt with here in detail. Let someone try for example to bring the 'thrownness' of existentialism into ontological agreement with the scientific picture of human development. Realization, on the contrary, produces both the genetic linkage and the basic ontological distinction and antithesis. The activity of man as a natural being gives rise, on the basis of inorganic and organic being, and proceeding from them, to a specifically new, more complicated and complex level of being, i.e., social being. (Nothing fundamental is changed in this overall situation by the fact that already in antiquity individual major thinkers reflected on the specificity of practice and the accomplished realization of the new it accomplishes, recognizing very pertinently some of its determinations.)

Realization as a category of the new form of being has a further important consequence. With labour, human consciousness ceases to be an epiphenomenon, in the ontological sense. It is true that the consciousness of animals, particularly the higher ones, seems to be an undeniable fact, but it is still a pale partial aspect serving a biologically based reproduction process which runs its course according to biological laws. And moreover this is not just the case with the reproduction of the species, where it is quite self-evident that the process takes place without any conscious intervention—according to laws that we have still not grasped scientifically today, but can only take cognizance of as an ontological fact; the same is also true of the reproduction of the individual. This we begin to grasp once we start to understand animal consciousness as a product of biological differentiation, of the growing complexity of organisms. The relationship of interaction between primitive organisms and their environment take place predominantly on the basis of biophysical and biochemical laws. The higher and more complicated an animal organism, the more it needs finer and more differentiated organs to maintain it in its interaction with its environment and reproduce itself. Here is not the place to depict this development, even in outline (and the present author does not consider himself competent to do so); but it is necessary to point out that the gradual development of animal consciousness from biophysical and biochemical reactions via stimuli and reflexes transmitted by the nervous system up to the highest level attained remains throughout locked into the framework of biological reproduction. It certainly displays an ever growing elasticity in reactions to the environment and to its possible changes; and this is shown very clearly with certain domestic animals and with experiments on apes. But it should not be forgotten, as has already been pointed out, that the initiative and direction in all these, the introduction of 'tools', etc., always comes from the human side, never from the animals themselves. Animal consciousness in nature never rises above the better serving of biological existence and reproduction, so that ontologically considered, it is an epiphenomenon of organic being.

Only in labour, in the positing of a goal and its means, consciousness rises with a self-governed act, the teleological positing, above mere adaptation to the environment—a stage retained by those animal activities that alter nature objectively but not deliberately—and begins to effect changes in nature itself that are impossible coming from nature alone, indeed even inconceivable. Since realization thus becomes a transforming and new-forming principle of nature, consciousness, which has provided the impulse and direction for this, can no longer be simply an ontological epiphenomenon. It is with this contention that dialectical materialism cuts itself off from mechanical materialism. For the latter recognizes only nature and its laws as objective reality. Marx carried through most decidedly the separation of the new materialism from the old, dialectical from mechanical, in his well-known *Theses on Feuerbach:* 'The chief defect of all previous materialism (that of Feuerbach included) is that things, reality, sensuousness are conceived only in the form of the *object, or of contemplation,* but not as *sensuous human activity, practice,* not subjectively. Hence, in contradistinction to materialism, the *active* side was set forth abstractly by idealism—which, of course, does not know real, sensuous activity as such. Feuerbach wants sensuous objects, really distinct from conceptual objects, but he does not conceive human activity itself as *objective* activity.' He goes on to state quite clearly that the reality of thought, which is no longer the epiphenomenal character of consciousness, can only be discovered and demonstrated in practice: 'The dispute over the reality or non-reality of thinking which is isolated from practice is a purely *scholastic* question.'[13] If we have here depicted labour as the original form of practice, this corresponds completely to the spirit of Marx's position; Engels, too, saw the decisive motor of man's humanization precisely in labour, some several decades later. Of course this contention on our part is so far no more than a declaration of principle, even if one which when correctly stated already contains and even illuminates several decisive determinations of the complex objectivity. But it is self-evident that this truth can only demonstrate and prove itself as such by being made as complete and explicit as possible. Even the mere fact that in the world of reality, realizations (the results of human practice in labour) appear as new forms of objectivity not derivable from nature, yet which are just as much realities as the products of nature are, bears witness at this initial level to the correctness of our contention.

We shall have much to say, both in this chapter and those following, about the concrete modes of appearance and expression of consciousness, and about the concrete mode of being of its no longer epiphenomenal property. For the moment, only the basic problem can be signalled, and to start with only in an extremely abstract way. What is involved here is the inseparable correlation of two acts that are in themselves mutually heterogenous, but which in their new ontological linkage compose the specific existing complex of labour, and as we shall see, form the ontological foundation of social practice, even of social being in general. These two heterogenous acts we are referring to here are, on the one hand, the precisest possible reflection of the reality in question, and on the other hand the subjoined positing of those causal chains which are indispensable, as we know, for the realization of the teleological positing. This first description of the phenomenon will show that two modes of considering reality that are heterogenous from one another form the basis of the ontological specificity of social being, both each for itself and in the indispensable combination of the two. If we now start our analysis with the reflection, this immediately shows a precise demarcation between objects that exist independent of the subject, and subjects that depict these objects with a greater or lesser degree of approximation, by acts of consciousness, to make them their own mental possession. This deliberately made separation between subject and object is a necessary product of the labour process, and at the same time the basis of the specifically human mode of existence. If the subject, separated from the object world as it is in consciousness, were unable to consider this object world and reproduce it in its inherent being, the positing of goals that underlies even the most primitive labour could not come about at all. Animals, too, of course, stand in a certain relationship to their environment, and one which becomes ever more complicated, ultimately mediated by a kind of consciousness. But since this relationship remains in the realm of the biological, no separation and confrontation of subject and object can arise in their case, as it does arise in man. Animals react with great certainty to whatever is useful or dangerous to them in their accustomed environment. I once read for example of a certain species of Asian wild goose which were not only able to recognize any birds of prey from a distance, but also to distinguish accurately between their various species and react to the different species differentially. It in no way follows from this that they distinguish these species conceptually, as man does. It is extremely questionable whether in completely different situations, if for example these birds of prey were brought close to them experimentally, and shown them in a peaceable state, they would have been in any way able to identify them with the distant image and the impending danger. The attempt to apply categories of human consciousness to the animal world, which is invariably arbitrary, leads at most to the conclusion that the higher animals can in the best of cases form pictorial representations of the most important elements of their environment; they can never form concepts of these. Of course, this term 'representation' must be used with the necessary reservation, for once a conceptual world has already been constructed, it reacts back again on perception and representation. This change, too, originally takes place under the influence of labour. Gehlen is quite right to point that in the human case there is a kind of division of labour of the senses in perception, so that man is in a position to perceive by vision alone certain properties of things which, as a biological being, he could only grasp by the sense of touch.[14]

Later on we shall have a lot more to say about the further consequences of this direction of development induced in man by labour. For the moment we must confine ourselves, for the purpose of clearly elaborating the new fundamental structure arising through labour, to indicating how the reflection of reality, as a precondition for the end and means of labour, gives rise to a separation, a freeing of man from his environment, a distancing, which is clearly revealed in the confrontation of subject and object. In the reflection of reality, the depiction is severed from the reality depicted, and channelled into a 'reality' of its own in consciousness. If we have put the word 'reality' in apostrophes here, it is because in consciousness the reality is merely reproduced. A new form of objectivity arises, but not a reality, and precisely from the ontological standpoint, it is impossible to equate the reproduction with what it reproduces, let alone identify the two. On the contrary. Ontologically, social being divides into two heterogenous moments, which not only confront one another as heterogenous from the standpoint of being, but are in fact actual antitheses: being and its reflection in consciousness.

This duality is a fundamental fact of social being. The earlier stages of being, by comparison, are strictly unitary. But the permanent and indispensable relationship of the reflection to being, its effect on being already in labour, and still more pronouncedly in further mediations (which we shall come on later), the determination of the reflection by its object, and so on, cannot fully abolish this duality. It is with this duality that man rises out of the animal world. In describing the second signalling system that is peculiar to man, Pavlov correctly maintained that only this system can get separated from reality, and go wrong in reproducing it. This is only possible because reflection here is oriented to the total object independent of consciousness, which is always and intensively an infinite one, seeking to grasp the object as it is in itself. It is precisely because of the necessary and self-imposed distance this involves that it can go astray. This is evidently not related only to the initial stages of reflection. Even when complicated ancillary constructions for grasping reality by reflection have

already developed, constructions that are inherently closed
and homogenous such as mathematics, geometry, logic, etc.,
the same possibility of error persists unchanged, still as the
result of this distancing. Certain possibilities of rudimentary
error may well be relatively excluded, but more complicated
ones then emerge in their place, precisely brought about by
the more distanced systems of mediation. It also follows from
this distancing and objectification that images can never be
quasi-photographic and mechanically faithful copies of reality.
They are always conditioned by the posited goals, and thus
genetically speaking by the social reproduction of life,
originally by labour. In my book *The Specificity of the
Aesthetic* I have indicated this concrete teleological orientation of reflection in analysing everyday thinking. We could
even say that this is the source of its fertility, its permanent
tendency to discover the new, while the objectification just
described is active as a corrective in the opposite direction.
As always with complexes, the result is the product of the
interaction of opposites. Yet up to now we have not yet
taken the decisive step towards understanding the ontological
relationship between reflection and reality. Reflection, here,
has a quite specific contradictory position. On the one hand
it is the strict antithesis of any being, and precisely because
it is reflection, it is not being; on the other hand and
simultaneously it is the vehicle for the rise of the new
objectivity in social being, and for its reproduction at the
same or a higher level. In this way, the consciousness that
reflects reality acquires a certain possibilistic character. As we
may recall, Aristotle championed the view that a builder,
even when he is not building, still remains an architect in
potentiality (δύναμις), while Hartmann refers to the
unemployed man for whom this potentiality reveals the
reality of his idle condition, i.e., that he is not in a position
to work. Hartmann's example is very instructive, as it shows
how the man in question, under the spell of one-sided and

narrow conceptions, can fail to realize the real underlying problem. It is undoubtedly the case, in other words, that in a major economic crisis many workers have no practical possibility of obtaining work; but it is similarly unquestionable—and here lies the profound inkling of truth in Aristotle's conception of *dynamis*—that at any time, should economic conditions improve, this man is ready to take up his former trade. How else then should this situation be defined, from the standpoint of an ontology of social being, than that he remains by his *dynamis* a worker, as a result of his upbringing, his former activity and experience, even when he is unemployed? This in no way leads to Hartmann's fear of a 'ghostly existence of possibility', for the unemployed man (with this real impossibility of finding work) is just as much an existing potential worker as in the case when his attempt to find work is realized. The upshot of this question is that Aristotle, with his broad, profound, universal and many-sided attempt to grasp the whole of reality in philosophy, perceives certain phenomena correctly, whereas Hartmann, as a result of being trapped in logical and epistemological insights into certain problems. If this category of possibility often leads to confusion with Aristotle, on account of his wrong views about the teleological character of society as a whole, and also of non-social reality, this does not essentially alter our conclusion, if we are out to distinguish the ontologically real from mere projections in forms of being that are not teleological in character. We could even say, in fact, that the required skills of the unemployed worker remain properties of his just as much as do other properties of any other existing thing; such properties may often persist, in organic nature for example, for very long periods of time, without being in any way actually effective, yet while remaining properties of the existence in question. We have already frequently pointed out the connection between property and possibility. This might be sufficient to refute

Hartmann's view, but it would not be sufficient to grasp the specific peculiarity of the possibility that is displayed here, and to which Aristotle's conception of *dynamis* is directed. Interestingly enough, we can find the point of departure for this precisely in Hartmann's work. In his analysis of biological being he points out, as we have already noted, that an organism's capacity for adaptation depends on its 'lability', as Hartmann describes this property. It is irrelevant here that Hartmann does not touch on the problem of possibility in dealing with this question. We could of course also describe this characteristic of an organism as its property, and declare the problem of possibility as settled in this way, as far as the present case is concerned. But this would be to miss the nub of our present question. The issue is not that this lability cannot at first be recognized in advance, but can only be established *post festum*, for the question as to whether something (in the ontological sense) can be recognized is immaterial to whether it is an actual existence in this respect. (The ontological reality of the simultaneity of two events has nothing to do with whether we are able to measure this simultaneity.)

By putting the question in this way, our answer to this ontological problem is that reflection, precisely from the ontological point of view, is not a being in itself; and as simply not a being at all, it is also not a 'ghostly existence'. And yet it is undoubtedly the decisive precondition for the positing of causal series, and precisely so in the ontological sense rather than that of epistemology. It is the ontological paradox that this gives rise to which Aristotle's conception of *dynamis*, with its dialectical rationality, seeks to illuminate. Aristotle correctly recognizes the ontological characteristic of the teleological positing, when he brings the essence of this into an inseparable connection with the conception of *dynamis*, since he defines *dynamis* or 'potency' as 'the principle enabling a thing to effect change or movement successfully, i.e., according to intention', making this definition more concrete as follows:

'It is on the strength of this principle by which the passive thing is affected that we call it capable of being affected either (i) in general or (ii) for the better. [Potency means, further] (2) the principle enabling a thing to effect change or movement successfully, i.e., according to intention. We sometimes say of a man who can walk or speak, but who cannot do so as well as he intended, that he *cannot* walk or speak.'[15]

Aristotle sees his way clearly through all ontological paradoxes of this kind; he maintains that 'actuality is prior to potency both in definition and in substance', and indicates very decisively the problem of modality that thus arises: 'Every potency is at the same time a potency of the opposite; for while that which is not capable of happening at all cannot happen to any subject, everything which is capable may fail to be actualized. Everything which is capable of being may either be or not be; it is therefore capable of being or not being.'[16] It would lead us into a labyrinth of unproductive scholasticism to demand of Aristotle that he should now 'derive' with compelling logic the 'necessity' of the constellation that he has so well depicted. This is impossible on principle with so eminently a purely ontological question as this. Certain confusions arise throughout in Aristotle's writings, bringing sham derivations in their wake, when he tries to extend what he has recognized here so well beyond the realm of human practice. What we are faced with today, and what Aristotle was also already faced with, was the phenomenon of labour in its uniqueness as the key category, dynamic and complex, of a newly arising level of being, and this confronts us in a clearly analysable form. The question now is to reveal this dynamic structure as a complex, by appropriate ontological analysis, so that, following Marx's own model, in which the human anatomy provides the key to the anatomy of the ape, we can at least make comprehensible the abstract-categorical path that has led up to this. It seems highly probable that the lability, in the biological sense, of the higher animals, whose significance has been explained by Hartmann, might provide a certain basis for labour. The development of domestic animals, standing as they do in a constant and intimate connection with humans, shows what great possibilities may be contained in this lability. Yet it must be stressed at the same time that this lability only forms a general basis, and that it is only by a leap that the most developed form of this phenomenon can form the basis for the transition to genuine human existence, a leap that is involved in the positing activity of even the most primitive man, still in the transition from animality. This leap can only be made comprehensible after the event, even if important advances in thought, such as this new form of possibility in Aristotle's conception of *dynamis,* shed a good deal of light on the path thus recognizable.

The transition from reflection as a special form of non-being to the active and productive being of the positing of causal relationships offers a developed form of Aristotelian *dynamis,* and one that we can define as the alternative character of any positing in the labour process. This first makes itself apparent with the positing of the goal of labour. If primitive man selects one stone out of a heap of stones as seemingly suitable for his purposes, and lets the others lie, it is clear that a choice or alternative is involved here. And an alternative, moreover, precisely in the sense that the stone, as an inherently existing object of inorganic nature, was in no way pre-formed to become an instrument for this positing. Of course, neither does grass grow to be eaten by cattle, or cattle to provide food for predators. But in both of these cases, the respective animals and their food are linked biologically, and their behaviour accordingly determined with biological necessity. The consciousness that emerges in their cases is thus unambiguously a determined one: an epiphenomenon, never an alternative. The stone selected as an instrument, however, is chosen by an act of consciousness that is no longer biological in character. By observation and experience, i.e., by reflection and the operations of consciousness, certain properties of the stone have to be recognized which make it suitable or unsuitable for the planned activity. What appears from outside as an extremely simple and unitary act, the selection of a stone, is most complicated and full of contradictions in its internal structure. What is involved here, in fact, are two alternatives, related but heterogeneous. Firstly, is the stone chosen right or wrong for the posited purpose? And secondly, is the goal posited correctly or otherwise, i.e., is a stone of any kind a really appropriate instrument for the posited goal? It is easy to see that both alternatives can only arise from a dynamically functioning and dynamically elaborated system of reflections of reality (i.e., from a system of acts that have no inherent being). But it is equally easy to see that if the results of the non-existing reflection congeal into an alternatively structured practice of this kind, then from the merely natural existence there can develop an existence in the framework of social being, for example a knife or an axe, i.e., a fully and radically new form of objectivity. For the stone in its natural existence and being-as-it-is *(Sosein)* has nothing at all to do with a knife or an axe.

The specificity of the alternative emerges still more transparently at a somewhat more developed level, i.e., if the stone is not only selected and used as an instrument of labour, but is subjected to a further process of preparation in order to be a better means of labour. Here, where labour is performed in a still more proper sense of the term, the alternative reveals its true nature still more clearly. It is not a once only act of decision, but rather a process, a continuous temporal chain of ever new alternatives. We only need reflect for a brief moment on any labour process, be it ever so rudimentary, to see that what is involved is never simply the

32

mechanical accomplishment of a posited goal. In nature, the chain of causality elapses 'automatically', following its own internal necessity of 'if. . . then'. In labour, however, as we have seen, not only is the goal teleologically posited, but the causal chain that realizes it must also be transformed into a posited causality. For both means and object of labour are in themselves natural things subject to natural causality, and it is only in the teleological positing, only by way of this, that they can receive the positedness of social existence in the labour process, even though they still remain natural objects. For this reason, the alternative is continuously repeated in the details of the labour process. Each individual movement in the process of sharpening, grinding, etc., must be considered correctly (i.e., must be based on a correct reflection of reality), be correctly oriented to the posited goal, correctly carried out by hand, etc. If this is not the case, then the posited causality can cease at any moment to be effective, and the stone once again becomes a simple natural existence subject to natural causalities, and having nothing more to do with means or object of labour. The alternative thus extends to that of a correct or mistaken activity for calling into being categories that only become forms of reality in the labour process.

Naturally, of course, mistakes can be of very different degree. They may be susceptible of correction by a subsequent act or acts, which again introduces new alternatives in the chain of decision (and the correction may be easy or difficult, depending on its variable interpolation in an act or series of acts); or else the mistake once made may vitiate the entire work. Thus alternatives in the labour process are not all of the same kind or status. What Churchill well said for the far more complicated cases of social practice, that one single decision may lead to a whole 'period of consequences', already appears in the most rudimentary form of labour as a characteristic of the structure of any social practice. This ontological structure of the labour process as a chain of alternatives should not be obscured by the way that in the course of development, and already so at relatively low levels, particular alternatives in the labour process can become conditioned reflexes, by practice and habit, and therefore can be carried out 'unconsciously'. Without going into the characteristics and functioning of conditioned reflexes here, and these are to be found also at more complicated levels, not only in labour itself but also in all fields of social practice—the contradictory character of routine, etc.—we must make clear that any conditioned reflex must originally have been the object of a decision between alternatives, both in the development of mankind as a whole and in that of each individual, who may well pick up these conditioned reflexes only by learning, practice, etc. At the beginning of this process there is precisely the chain of alternatives.

The alternative, therefore, which is likewise an act of consciousness, is a category of mediation, with the aid of which the reflection of reality becomes the vehicle for the positing of an existence. It must be stressed in this connection that this existence in labour is always something natural, and this natural property that it has can never be completely abolished. However great the transforming effects of the teleological positing of causalities in the labour process, the natural boundary can only retreat, it can never fully disappear; and this refers to the nuclear reactor as much as to the stone axe. For, to mention only one of the possibilities that emerge here, while natural causalities may well be subjected to those posited in labour, they never cease to be quite fully operative, since every natural object bears within it an intensive infinity of properties as its possibilities. Since their effectiveness stands in complete heterogeneity to the teleological positing, this must in many cases produce results that are opposed to the teleological positing and sometimes even destroy it (the corrosion of iron, etc.). The upshot of this is that the alternative must remain in operation even after the labour process in question is completed, in the form of checking, control, repair, etc., and these preventive .positings can only continuously increase the alternatives involved in the positing of goals and their realization. The development of labour, therefore, brings it about that the alternative character of human practice, the behaviour of man to his environment and to himself, comes to be based ever more strongly on decisions between alternatives. The overcoming of animality by the leap to humanization in labour, the overcoming of the epiphenomenal consciousness determined merely by biology, thus acquires, through the development of labour, an unstayable momentum, a tendency towards a prevalent universality. Here too we can see that the new forms of being can only develop gradually into really prevailing universal determinations of their own sphere. In the transitional leap, and for a long while after, they stand in constant competition with the lower forms of being from which they arose and which form their insuperable material basis, even when the transformation process has already reached a very high level.

Looking back from this point, the *dynamis* discovered by Aristotle as a new form of possibility can be assessed in its full significance. For the fundamental positing of both goal and means of accomplishment receives ever more strongly in the course of development a specifically fixed form, which can lead to the illusion that it was already a social being by its own inherent nature. Take, for example, a modern factory. The model for it (the teleological positing) is elaborated, discussed, costed, etc., before it can actually go into production, and this often involves a very large collective. Even though the material existence of many people is based on the elaboration of models of this kind, even though the process of model-making generally has a significant material foundation (offices,* equipment, etc.), the model still remains a possibility, in Aristotle's sense, and can only become reality by the decision to go ahead with the plan, a decision based on

35

alternatives, just as with primitive man's decision to choose this stone or that to use as a hatchet or axe. Indeed, the alternative character of the decision to realize the teleological positing contains still further complications, which however only emphasize the more sharply its significance as a leap from possibility to reality. Consider how for primitive man it was only immediate usefulness that was the object of the alternative, while with the developing social character of production, i.e., of the economy, the alternatives take on an ever more ramified and differentiated form. The development of technology itself has the result that the plan of the model must be the outcome of a chain of alternatives, but no matter how high the level of development of technology (its support by a whole series of sciences), this cannot be the sole ground for decision between alternatives. For the technical optimum worked out in this way in no way coincides immediately with the economic optimum. Economy and technique may well be inseparably coexistent in the development of labour, standing in a permanent relationship of mutual interaction, but this in no way abolishes their heterogeneity, which as we have seen, is displayed in the contradictory dialectic of end and means; often it even strengthens this contradictory character. This heterogeneity, whose complicated moments we cannot go into here, has the consequence that while labour may well have created science as an ancillary organ for its ever higher and more social realization, the interaction of the two can only ever be realized in an uneven development.

If we now consider a project of this kind ontologically, it is clear to see that it bears within it the essential character of Aristotle's 'potency': 'Everything which is capable of being may either be or not be; it is therefore capable of being or not being.' In precisely the same sense as Aristotle, Marx says that the instrument of labour 'has, likewise, transposed itself from mere possibility into a reality' in the course of the labour process.[17] No matter how complicated a project might be, and even if it is drawn up on the basis of correct reflections, if it is rejected, it remains a non-existence, even though it contained the possibility within it of becoming an existence. It remains the case, in this connection, that it is only the alternative of that man (or that collective of men) who is called on to set in motion the process of material realization by labour, that can effect this transformation of potential into existence. This not only shows the upper limit of this kind of possibility, to become real, but also its lower limit, which determines when and to what extent a reflection of reality consciously oriented towards realization can become a possibility in this sense. This limit of possibility can in no way be reduced to the level of thought—the exactitude, originality, etc., of simple reason. Naturally, in the last analysis the aspects of the projected goal to be posited for labour play an important role in the decision between alternatives; but it would be to fetishize economic reason if we were to see in it alone the motor for the leap from possibility to reality in the area of labour. A reason of this kind is a myth, just as is the assumption that the alternatives we have described are accomplished at a level of abstract and pure freedom. In both cases we must bear in mind that the alternatives bearing on labour always press for decision under concrete conditions, again irrespective of whether what is involved is the production of a stone axe or the prototype of a car that will then be produced in a hundred thousand copies. The first consequence of this is that rationality is based on the concrete need that the particular product has to satisfy. The components that determine this satisfaction of needs, and hence also the ideas made of it, thus also define the construction of the project, the selection and arrangement of perspectives, as well as the attempt to reflect correctly the causal relations involved in the realization; in the last analysis, therefore, the definition is founded in the particular characteristics of the planned realization. Its rationality can therefore never be an absolute one, but as with all attempts to realize something, simply the concrete rationality of an 'if... then' connection. The fact that necessary connections of this kind prevail within such a framework is what makes the alternative into something possible. Within this concrete complex, it presupposes the necessary succession of individual steps. It might well be objected that since alternative and predetermination logically exclude one another, the alternative must precisely have its ontological foundation in the freedom of decision. This is correct up to a certain point, but only up to this point. To understand it correctly, we must bear in mind that whichever side it is viewed from, the alternative can only be a concrete one: the decision of a concrete person (or group of people) as to the best concrete conditions of realization for a concretely posited goal. It follows from this that an alternative (or any chain of alternatives) in labour never refers to reality in general; it is a concrete selection between ways to realize a goal that has not been produced by a subject deciding for himself, but rather by the social being in which he lives and acts. It is only out of this complex of being that exists and is determined independently of him that the subject can rise through these determined possibilities to the object of the goal he posits, to his alternative. And it is equally illuminating to note that the space for decision is similarly defined by this complex of being; it is self-evident that scope and profundity, etc., in the correct reflection of reality play a weighty role here, but this does not alter the fact that even the positing of causal series within the teleological positing—whether direct or mediated—is ultimately determined by social being itself.

The fact of course remains that any concrete decision about a teleological positing can never be completely derived, with rigorous necessity,* from its antecedent conditions. On the other hand, however, it must be remembered that when we consider not the individual isolated act of teleological positing, but rather the totality of these acts and their mutual relations with one another in a given society, we inevitably come to establish tendential similarities, convergences, types, etc. The proportion of these convergent or divergent tendencies in this totality shows the reality of the concrete space for teleological positing that we have just indicated. The real social process, from which arises not only the positing of the goal but also the discovery and application of the means, defines precisely the concretely limited space for possible questions and answers, for alternatives that can actually be realized. The determining components appear still more concretely and firmly defined in the existing totality than in the individual acts of positing when these are considered in isolation. Yet this is still to present only one side of the alternative. No matter how clearly defined the description of this space for manoeuvre, it cannot abolish the fact that the act of the alternative contains a moment of decision, a choice, and that the 'place' and organ of this decision is human consciousness. It is precisely this ontologically real function that lifts this consciousness above the epiphenomenon of animal consciousness, which is completely conditioned by biology.

In a certain sense, therefore, we could speak here of the ontological kernel of freedom that has played, and still does play, so great a role in philosophical disputes about man and society. But the essential character of such an ontological genesis of freedom, which appears for the first time in reality in the alternative within the labour process, still has to be made more clear and concrete, so as not to give rise to any misunderstanding. If we conceive labour in its essential original nature—as the producer of use-values—as an 'eternal' form that persists through the change in social formations, i.e., the metabolism between man (society) and nature, it is then clear that the intention that defines the character of the alternative is directed towards a change in natural objects, even though it is induced by social needs. In discussing this subject we have so far been concerned to stress this original characteristic of labour and to save for later analysis its more developed and complicated forms, which already arise with the socio-economic positing of exchange-value and its interactions with use-values. It is only possible with difficulty, of course, to consistently establish this level of abstraction throughout in Marx's sense, without introducing for the purpose of particular analyses facts that already presuppose more concrete conditions determined by the particular society in question. Thus, when we referred above to the heterogeneity of the technical and the economic optimum, we only embarked on such an expansion of the field of view in order to indicate the complexity of the elements involved in the transformation of possibility into reality with reference to a concrete example— as a kind of horizon, as it were. Now, however, we must deal with labour exclusively in the most narrow sense of the word, in its rudimentary form, as the organ of the metabolism between man and nature. For it is only in this way that we can exhibit those categories that are given with ontological necessity by this rudimentary form, and which therefore make labour a model for social practice in general. It will be the task of subsequent investigations, for the most part only in our Ethics, to exhibit those complications, qualifications, etc., that arise on the basis of a society grasped ever more strongly in its developed totality.

Understood in this way, labour presents a double visage ontologically. On the one hand it is illuminating at this level of generality that practice is only possible as a result of the teleological positing of a subject, but that a positing of this kind involves a knowledge and a positing of natural causal processes as positings. On the other hand, what is principally involved is a relationship of interaction between man and nature, of such a kind that it is correct in analysing the positing only to pay heed to the categories arising from this. We shall see straight away that even when we turn to consider the changes that labour brings about in its subject, the specific character of this relationship which we perceive dominates the nature of the newly arisen categories, so that the other extremely important transformations in the subject are already the products of more developed stages, and from the social point of view higher ones, which of course must still have their original form in simple labour as the ontological precondition. We have seen how the decisive new category that brings about the leap from possibility to reality is precisely the alternative. What then is its ontological content? It sounds somewhat surprising when first stated if we indicate as its dominant moment its principally epistemological character. Of course, the first impulse to the teleological positing is the desire for the satisfaction of needs. But this is still a common feature of both human and animal life. The parting of the ways only sets in when the teleological positing is interpolated between the need and its satisfaction. In this simple circumstance, which contains the first impulse for labour, we have clear expression of its characteristic as predominantly epistemological, for it is undoubtedly a victory of conscious behaviour over the mere spontaneity of biological instinct when labour intervenes as a mediation between the need and its immediate satisfaction.

This situation is even more clearly shown when the mediation is realized in the chain of alternatives associated with labour. Man in his labour must necessarily seek success for his activity. But he can only obtain this if both in the positing of goals and in the selection of means towards them, he directs himself undeviatingly to grasping everything connected with his labour in its objective being-in-itself, and behaves appropriately towards both goal and means. What is involved in this is not only the intention of objective reflection, but also the attempt to exclude everything merely instinctive, emotional, etc., that might obscure objective insight. This is the very way in which consciousness comes to be dominant over instinct, knowledge over mere emotion. This does not of course mean that the labour of primitive man, as it arose, took place in the forms of present-day consciousness. The forms of consciousness in question are certainly different from this in quality, in a way that we are not even in a position to reconstruct. Yet it pertains to the objective preconditions of labour's existence, as we have already shown, that only a correct reflection of reality, as it is in itself, independent of consciousness, can accomplish the realization of the posited goal in the face of indifferent and heterogenous natural causalities, transforming these into posited causalities that serve the teleological positing. The concrete alternatives of labour in the determination of its goals and in their achievement thus involve in the last analysis a choice between the correct and the incorrect. This is what constitutes their ontological nature, their power of transforming the Aristotelian *dynamis* into a concrete realization. This primary character of the knowledge aspect is the labour alternative is thus an insuperable fact, precisely the ontological facticity *(Geradesosein)* of labour. This can therefore be recognized quite independent of the forms of consciousness in which it was originally—and perhaps for a long time after realized.

This transformation of the working subject—the genuine humanization of man—is the necessary ontological consequence of this objective facticity of labour. In his definition of labour, the text of which we have already quoted, Marx also speaks of its decisive effect on the human subject. He shows how by acting on nature, man changes himself, and 'in this way he simultaneously changes his own nature. He develops the potentialities slumbering within nature, and subjects the play of its forces to his own sovereign power.'[18] What this means above all, and we shall already have to discuss this in the objective analysis of labour, is the mastery of consciousness over mere biological instinct. Considered from the standpoint of the subject, the upshot of this is an ever repeated continuity of this mastery, and moreover a continuity which must emerge in each individual movement of labour, as a new problem, a new alternative, ending each time that labour is successful with the victory of correct understanding over mere instinct. For in the same way that the natural being of the stone stands in complete heterogeneity to its use as a knife or an axe, and can undergo this transformation only as a result of the positing by man of a correctly recognized causal chain, so it stands also in heterogenous relationship with the original biologically instinctive movements of man himself. Man must devise his movements expressly for the work in hand, and execute these in constant struggle against mere instinct in himself, against himself. Here, too, we can see Aristotle's *dynamis* (Marx uses the term *'Potenz'* [potentiality], also favoured by Prantl, the historian of logic) as the categorical expression of this transition. What Marx refers to here as 'potentiality' is in the last analysis the same thing as N. Hartmann describes as lability in the biological being of the higher animals, a great elasticity in adaptation, even to basically different circumstances if necessary. This was certainly the biological basis for the transformation of a certain higher animal into man. And we can observe the same thing with higher animals in captivity, and domestic animals. But this elastic behaviour, this actualization of potentialities, remains in that case purely biological, since the demands on the animal are made from outside, governed by man, as a new environment in the broadest sense of the term, so that here consciousness necessarily remains an epiphenomenon. Labour, however, as already emphasized, signals a leap in this development. Not only does adaptation pass from the instinctual to the conscious, but it develops as an 'adaptation' to circumstances that are not created by nature, but are self-selected, self-created.

This is the very reason why 'adaptation' in the case of

working man is not internally stable and static as with other
living beings, which are generally accustomed to reacting to an
unchanged environment in the same way, and not to one
controlled from outside as domestic animals are. The element
of self-creation not only alters the environment itself, and
this not only in a directly material way but also in its material
reactions on man; so that as a result of labour, for example,
the sea, which originally was a barrier to movement, came to
be an ever more frequented means of connection. Over and
above this—and of course giving rise to such changes of
function—this structural property of labour reacts back also
on the working subject. If we are to understand the resulting
transformations in the subject correctly, we must proceed
from the objective situation already described, i.e., that the
subject is the initiator of the posited goal, of the transformation of reflected causal chains into posited ones, of the
realizing of all these positings in the labour process. What is
involved here is therefore a whole series of different positings,
both of a theoretical and a practical kind, by the subject. The
common element in all of these, if we are out to comprehend
them as acts of a subject, is that in every case what can be
grasped immediately by instinct is replaced or at least mastered
by acts of consciousness, as a result of the distancing that is
necessarily involved in every positing. We should not get led
astray here by the appearance that in any task that is
habitually practised, most of the individual acts involved no
longer possess a directly conscious character. What is
'instinctive' and 'unconscious' in them is based on the
transformation of movements that arose consciously into
established conditioned reflexes. It is not primarily in this way
that these are distinguished from the instinctive behaviour
of the higher animals, but rather that what is no longer
conscious here is something that is permanently recallable.
It is the accumulated experience of labour that has established
it as a reflex, and new experience can at any time replace it

by new movements that are similarly established until recall. The accumulation of labour experience thus follows a double line of cancellation and preservation of the habitual movements, in such a way that, even if these are fixed as conditioned reflexes, they always contain within them their origin in the distanced positing that determines end and means, and checks and corrects the execution.

A further important consequence of this distancing is that man is compelled in his labour to consciously master his emotions. He may become tired, but if an interruption would harm his work, he must still continue it; he may be struck by fear, as for example in hunting, but must still hold his ground and continue the struggle with strong and dangerous animals. (It should be stressed here again that we are assuming labour performed for the sake of its use-values, which was certainly its initial form. It is only in far more complicated class societies that other motives originating in social being interfere with this original behaviour, e.g., sabotage. Here, too, however, the dominance of consciousness over instinct remains the basic orientation.) It is immediately evident that in this way modes of behaviour appear in human life which are of decisive importance for the genuine humanization of man. It is a matter of general knowledge that man's command over his instincts, emotions, etc., is the major problem of all morality, from custom and tradition through to the highest forms of ethics. The problems of the higher levels, of course, can only be dealt with later, and really adequately only in our own Ethics; but it is of decisive importance for the ontology of social being that they appear already at the most rudimentary stage of labour, and moreover in the quite distinct form of the conscious mastery of feelings, etc. Man has often been characterized as a tool-making animal. This is certainly true, but it must be added that the making and use of tools involves human self-control as here described as an indispensable precondition. This, too, is an aspect of the leap described here, the emergence of man from merely animal existence. If similar phenomena seem to appear with domestic animals, e.g., retrieving in the case of hunting dogs, it must be repeated yet again that habits of this kind can only arise in the human environment, and forced on the animal by man, whereas man achieves his own self-control as a necessary precondition for realizing his self-posited goals in labour. Thus it is also valid in this respect to say that labour is a vehicle for the self-production of man as man. As a biological being, man is a product of natural development. With his self-realization, which of course even in his case means only a retreat of the natural boundary, and never its disappearance, its complete conquest, he enters into a new and self-founded being, into social being.

2. *Labour as a Model for Social Practice*

Our arguments in the last section have shown how problems which at an advanced level of human development assume a very generalized, dematerialized, subtle and abstract form, and for this reason later come to constitute the major themes of philosophy, are already contained *in nuce,* in their most general but most decisive determinations, in the positings of the labour process. We believe therefore that it is right to see labour as the model for all social practice, all active social behaviour. As our intention in what follows is to present this essential character of labour in its relationships with categories of an extremely complicated and derivative kind, the reservations we have already stated with regard to the character of the labour we are assuming must be made still more concrete. We said that we would deal firstly only with labour as the producer of useful objects, use-values. The new functions that labour acquires with the rise of social production in the true sense of the term (the problems of exchange-value) are not yet present in our model representation, and will only be properly depicted in our next chapter.

Still more important, however, we must now point out what it is that distinguishes labour in this sense from the more developed forms of social practice. Labour in this original and narrow sense involves a process between human activity and nature: its acts are directed towards the transformation of natural objects into use-values. In the later and more developed forms of social practice, the effect on other people comes more to the fore, and ultimately—if only ultimately—this effect aims at the production of use-values. Here, again, the teleological positings and the posited causal series they set in train form the ontological and structuring foundation. The essential content of the teleological positing, however, is from now on (speaking very generally and in the abstract) the attempt to bring another man (or group of men) to accomplish specific teleological positings for their own part. This problem arises as soon as labour has become sufficiently social that it depends on cooperation between several people; independent, this time, of whether the problem of exchange-value has already arisen or whether the cooperation is oriented simply to use-value production. This second form of teleological positing, therefore, that in which the posited goal is directly the positing of a goal for other people, can already appear at a very rudimentary stage.

Let us consider hunting in the paleolithic era. The size, strength and danger of the animals hunted made the cooperation of a group necessary. But if this cooperation was to function successfully, there had to be a division of functions among the individual participants (beaters and hunters). The teleological positings that follow from this have a secondary character, from the standpoint of the immediate labour itself; they must be preceded by a teleological positing that defines the character, role, function, etc., of the individual concrete and real positings that are oriented to a natural object. The object of this secondary goal positing, therefore, is no longer something purely natural, but rather the consciousness of a human group; the posited goal is no longer designed directly to change a natural object, but rather to bring about a teleological positing that really is oriented to the natural objects. The means, likewise, are no longer directly effects on natural objects, but such as seek to induce such effects from other people.

Secondary teleological positings of this kind already stand much closer to the social practice of more developed stages than does the actual labour that we are assuming here. Their detailed analysis must wait until later. But the distinction itself had already to be indicated at this point. Partly because even the first glance at this higher social level of labour shows that labour in the sense previously considered forms its insurpassable real foundation, the final goal of a mediating chain of teleological positings that may be very ramified, and partly because the first glance at these connections also shows how out of the original labour more complicated forms of this kind must necessarily develop, from the dialectic of its own properties. And this double connection indicates a simultaneous identity and non-identity at the various levels of labour, even in the case of wide-ranging, multifold and complicated mediations.

We have seen already how the consciously-executed teleological positing brings about a distancing in the reflection of reality, and how it is only with this distancing that the subject-object relation arises, in the true sense of the term. Both simultaneously involve the rise of a conceptual grasp of the phenomena of the real world, and their adequate expression in language. If we want to understand correctly the genesis of these very complicated and intricate inter-actions, both in their initial rise and in their further develop-ment, we must proceed from the fact that everywhere that genuine changes of being take place, the total connection of the complex involved has primacy over its elements. These elements can only be comprehended in terms of their concrete collaboration within the particular complex of being in question, whereas it would be a vain task to try and reconstruct mentally the complex of being in terms of its elements. In this way one would end up with a pseudo-problem like the warning example of the scholastics, whether the hen is ontologically prior to the egg. Today one might almost take this as a mere joke; but it is worth considering whether the question as to whether the word arose out of the concept or vice versa is the least bit closer to reality, i.e., more reasonable. For word and concept, speech and conceptual thought belong together as elements of a complex, the complex of social being, and they can only be grasped in their true nature in the context of an ontological analysis of social being, by knowledge of the real functions that they fulfil within this complex. Naturally, of course, there is a predominant moment in any such system of interrelations within a complex of being, as indeed in any interaction. And this character arises in a purely ontological connection, without any kind of value hierarchy being involved. In inter-relationships of this kind the individual elements can either reciprocally condition one another, as in the present case of word and concept, in which case neither can exist without the other, or the kind of conditioning is such that one element forms the precondition for the other's appearance, and this relationship is not reversible. A genetic derivation of speech or conceptual thought from labour is certainly possible, since the execution of the labour process poses demands on the subject involved that can only be fulfilled simultaneously by the reconstruction of psychophysical abilities and possibilities that were already present into language and conceptual thought, whereas this cannot be understood ontologically without the antecedent requirements of labour, or even the conditions that gave rise to the genesis of the labour process. It goes without saying that once the needs of labour have given rise to speech and conceptual thought, their development must be an incessant and indissoluble interaction; the fact that labour continues to form the predominant moment in no way removes the permanent character of such interaction, but on the contrary strengthens and intensifies it. It necessarily follows from this that within a complex of this kind, there must be a continuous influence of labour on speech and conceptual thought, and vice versa.

Only this kind of conception of the ontological genesis as one of a concretely structured complex can shed light on the fact that this genesis is simultaneously both a leap (from the organic to the social) and a prolonged process lasting for millennia. The leap presents itself as soon as the new property of being is actually realized, even in the most rudimentary and isolated acts. But it is then an extremely lengthy development, for the most part inevitably full of contradictions and uneven, until the new categories of being extend in such a way, both extensively and intensively, that the new level of being manages to constitute itself as well defined and resting on its own basis.

As we have already seen, the essential feature of developments of this kind consists in the way that the categories specific and peculiar to the new complexes attain an ever stronger supremacy over the lower levels, even though materially these must permanently continue to be the basis of their existence. It is the same in the relationship of organic nature to inorganic as in that of social being to these two natural levels. This development of the categories unique to a new level of being always proceeds by their growing differentiation and with this also the increasing—if always simply relative—autonomy they acquire within the existing complexes of a form of being.

In social being this is most readily apparent with the forms in which reality is reflected. The fact that only a materially correct reflection (in connection with the concrete labour of the time) of the causal relations relevant to the goal of labour can achieve the transformation into posited causal relations that is unconditionally necessary, does not only act in the direction of a constant checking and perfection of the acts of reflection, but also leads to their generalization. Since experience gained in one concrete labour can be used in another, this experience gradually becomes relatively autonomous, i.e., certain observations are generalized and fixed, so that they are no longer exclusively related directly to one particular performance, but acquire a certain universal character as observations about natural processes in general. Such generalizations of this kind contain the kernels of future sciences, whose beginnings, like those of geometry and arithmetic, are lost in the distant past. Without having a clear awareness of this, certain generalizations that are in their most incipient stage can already contain decisive principles of later sciences that are by this time genuinely independent, e.g., the principle of disanthropomorphizing, of the abstractive consideration of determinations that are inseparably linked with human reactions to the environment (and also to man himself). These principles are already contained implicitly in the most rudimentary conceptions of arithmetic and geometry. And this is moreover quite independent of whether the people who work them out and use them are aware of their real nature or not. The stubborn linking of such concepts with magical and mythical ideas, which stretches far into historical time, shows how purposive and necessary action, its correct mental preparation and accomplishment, can mingle in human consciousness with false ideas of non-existent things as the true and final basis, yet still giving rise to ever higher forms of practice. This shows how consciousness of tasks, of the world, and of the subject itself grows out of the reproduction of his own existence (and with it that of the being of the species), as its indispensable instrument; it may well become ever more elaborate and independent, even very highly mediated, yet it is ultimately an instrument for this reproduction of man himself.

The problem of false consciousness which we have touched on here, and the possibility of its being for a time relatively correct and productive, can only be discussed adequately in a later connection. These considerations have simply led us to the paradoxical relationship in which human consciousness, called into being in labour, for labour, and by labour, intervenes in the activity of man's own reproduction. This could be expressed by saying that the independence of reflection of the external and internal world in human consciousness is an indispensable precondition for the rise and further development of labour. Science and theory as a self-acting and autonomous form of the original teleological and causal positings in labour, however, can never quite abandon this ultimate tie to their origin even at their highest level of development. Our later discussion will show how they never could lose this tie to the satisfaction of the needs of the human species, no matter how complicated and ramified the mediations that link them to this. In this double relationship of linkage and autonomy *(Aufsichselbstgestelltsein)* an important problem is also reflected, a problem which human consideration, humanity's consciousness and self-consciousness, is forced in the course of history to pose and answer time and again: the problem of theory and practice. And to find the correct way in to this complex of questions, we must turn back once again to a problem we have already touched on frequently, that of teleology and causality.

As long as the real problem of being in nature and history was conceived teleologically, with causality only being attributed the role of executive organ for the 'final purpose', theory, or contemplation, had to be seen as the highest form of human behaviour. For as long as the teleological character of reality was accepted as the unbreakable foundation of the essence of objective reality, the only relationship of man to this that was ultimately possible was a contemplative one; this seemed the only attitude to reality that would enable him to grasp and understand the specific problems of his life, both in the immediate sense and in the most subtly mediated. It is true that the teleologically posited character of human practice was recognized relatively early on. But since the concrete activities resulting from this still flowed into a teleologically conceived totality of nature and society, this philosophical, ethical, religious, etc., supremacy of the contemplative grasp of cosmic teleology still persisted. Here is not the place even to indicate the mental struggles to which such a view of the world gave rise. It should just be briefly noted that the top place of contemplation in the hierarchy was generally maintained even in those philosophies which had already taken up the struggle against the dominance of teleology in their cosmological ideas. The reason for this seems at first sight paradoxical. The complete dethronement of divinity from the external world was achieved less quickly than liberation from its teleological and theodictic properties. This meant that the intellectual passion oriented towards exposing the objective teleology with its religiously indicated subject often tended to drive out teleology altogether, which then hindered a concrete understanding of practice (labour). It was only in classical German philosophy that practice begun to be judged according to its true importance. As Marx says in criticism of the old materialism in the first *Thesis of Feuerbach* that we have already quoted: 'Hence, in contradistinction to materialism, the *active* side was set forth abstractly by idealism.' This opposition, which also contains a criticism of idealism in the word 'abstractly', is made concrete in the reproach that idealism 'of course, does not know real, sensuous activity as such'.[1] As we know, Marx's criticism of Hegel's *Phenomenology* in his *Economic and Philosophical Manuscripts* precisely focuses on the merit and limitation of German idealism, particularly that of Hegel.

Marx's position against both the old materialism and

against idealism is thus clearly defined. The solution of the problem of theory and practice requires reference back to practice in its real and material form of appearance, where its fundamental ontological .determinations are readily apparent and can be unambiguously perceived. What is so path-breaking in this way of posing the question for the development of human thought and world-view, in putting labour at the centre of this dispute, is not simply that any introjection of teleology is critically removed from the process of being in its totality, and that labour (social practice) is seen as the only complex of being in which the teleological positing is attributed a real and authentic role in changing reality; also established on this basis, but going far beyond it with a generalization that transcends the mere establishment of an ontologically fundamental fact, is the only philosophically correct relationship between teleology and causality. What is essential in this relationship, we have already presented in our analysis of the dynamic structure of labour. Teleology and causality are not, as they previously were for an analysis based on logic or epistemology, mutually exclusive principles in the course of processes, in the existence and facticity *(Sosein)* of things, but rather principles that, while heterogenous, only give rise to the ontological foundation of certain complexes of motion together, in inseparable coexistence for all their contradictoriness, and moreover, complexes which are only ontologically possible in the realm of social being, whose effectiveness in this, however, is at the same time that which produces the major characteristic of this level of being.

Also in our above analysis of labour, we have been able to establish a further and most important characteristic of these categorical determinations of movement. It pertains to the very nature of teleology that it can only really function as something posited. In order to define it in an ontologically concrete manner, therefore, it is necessary, if a process is to be rightly characterized as teleological, that the being of the positing subject should also be indicated ontologically in an unambiguous way. Causality, on the other hand, can operate both in a posited and in a non-posited way. A correct analysis, therefore, does not only require a precise distinction between these two modes of being, but also requires the liberation of posited being from any philosophical ambiguity. For in certain very influential philosophies—it is sufficient to indicate the Hegelian—the distinction between a merely epistemological positing of causality and a materially real, ontological one, becomes confused and disappears. If on the basis of earlier analyses we lay emphasis on the fact that it is exclusively a materially and ontologically posited causality that can maintain this relationship of coexistence with an always posited teleology, we are in no way reducing the importance of the positing of causality purely in knowledge. (The specifically epistemological or logical positing of causality is a further abstraction, and is therefore not at issue here.) On the contrary. Our earlier discussion has clearly shown that the ontological positing of concrete causal series presupposes their knowledge, and therefore their posited being as knowledge. It is simply that we should never lose sight of the fact that all that this positing can attain is a possibility, in the sense of the Aristotelian *dynamis,* while the transformation of potential into realization is a special act, which may well presuppose this but is heterogenous and distinct from it. This act is precisely the decision arising from the alternative.

The ontological coexistence of teleology and causality in working (practical) human behaviour, and here alone, has the result, as far as being is concerned, that by virtue of their social nature theory and practice must be elements of one and the same complex of social being, so that they can only be adequately understood on the basis of this reciprocal relationship. Precisely here, labour can serve as a model in the most illuminating way. This may sound somewhat surprising at first, for it is labour of all things that is in the most blatant manner teleologically oriented, the interest in the realization of the posited goal appearing most transparently. For all that, it is in labour, and in its acts that transform spontaneous causality into posited, that the pure knowledge-character of the acts involved is more purely maintained. This is because what is involved here is still exclusively a reciprocal relationship between man and nature, and not yet between man and man, man and society, as in actions of a more complex kind, in which social interests are inevitably involved already in the reflection of the facts. The acts by which causality is posited in labour are those most purely governed by the antithesis of true and false, for as we have already seen, any mistake about the causality that inherently exists in the process of its positing, must inevitably lead to the failure of the entire labour process. It is immediately evident, however, that in any positing of causality where the immediately posited goal is a change in the positing consciousness of other men, the social interest which is contained in any positing of goals—and of course even in that of simple labour—must inexorably influence even the positing of the causal series indispensable to the planned realization. This is all the more so in that in the case of labour itself even the positing of causal series is related to objects and processes which behave in their posited being with complete indifference to the posited goal, whereas those positings designed to effect certain decisions among alternatives in other men are at work in a material that spontaneously presses to alternative decisions of its own accord. This kind of positing aims therefore at a change, a strengthening or a weakening, of these tendencies in human consciousness, and operates as a consequence not in a material that is inherently indifferent, but rather in one that is already tendentially moved towards the positing of purposes, either favourably or unfavourably. Even the possible indifference of the men involved towards deliberate influencing of this kind has not more than the name in common with the above mentioned indifference of the natural material. For nature, this indifference is a metaphor designed to indicate its eternal and unchanging completely neutral heterogeneity in regard to human goals, whereas the indifference of men towards such intentions is a concrete form of behaviour, either social or individual, which can be changed in the appropriate circumstances.

In the positings of causality of a higher, more social kind, therefore, the intervening influence of the teleological positing on its mental reproductions is unavoidable. Even if this latter act has been constituted as science, as a relatively autonomous factor of social life, it is an illusion, ontologically speaking, to believe that it would be possible to attain a completely unprejudiced reproduction of the causal chains that prevail in this case, and in this way also one of natural causalities, or that a more pure form of immediate and exclusive confrontation between man and nature could be achieved here than in labour itself. Science does of course achieve a far more exact, wide-ranging, more profound and complete knowledge of the pertinent natural causalities than would ever be possible in labour simply on its own basis. This is a truism, but does not resolve our present problem. What is at issue here is that this advance in knowledge involves the loss of the exclusive counterposition of man and nature, and it must immediately be added in this connection that this very loss gives an impulse to progress. In labour, in other words, man is confronted with the being-in-itself of that section of nature which stands in direct connection with the goal of his labour. When this knowledge is raised to a higher level of generalization, which is already the case of a science developing towards independence, this is not possible without ontological categories of intention increasingly intervening in the reflection of nature, linked as these are with human social life. Naturally, this should not be taken in a vulgarly direct sense. Firstly, every teleological positing is ultimately socially determined by need, and that of labour in a very pregnant way, and no science can be completely free from this causative influence. This, however, would not yet amount to a decisive distinction. Secondly, though, science places the generalization of relationships in the centre of its disanthropomorphizing reflection of reality. We have seen how this no longer pertains directly to the ontological essence of labour, and particularly not to its genesis; all that is involved in this is the correct grasp of a concrete natural phenomenon, in as much as its characteristic properties stand in a necessary connection with the teleologically posited goal of labour. Labouring man may have the most erroneous ideas of the more mediated relationships; but these need not disturb the correct reflection of the immediate ones, and thereby the success of the labour process (the relationship of primitive labour to magic).

But as soon as reflection is directed towards generalizations, problems of a general ontology necessarily emerge, no matter whether consciously or not. And even if, where nature is concerned, these are quite separate from society and its needs, at least in their unadulterated and inherent form, completely neutral towards these, yet the ontology thereby brought to consciousness cannot remain indifferent towards any social practice, in the more mediated sense already investigated. The close connection between theory and practice has the necessary consequence that the latter, in its concrete and social forms of appearance, is influenced to a very profound extent by the ontological ideas that men hold about nature. Science, for its part, if it takes the adequate comprehension of reality seriously, can in no way escape these ontological questions. And whether this happens consciously or not, whether the questions and answers are true or false, whether it even denies the possibility of a rational answer to these questions, seems a matter of indifference at this level, for even this denial has some ontological effect on social consciousness. And since social practice always unfolds in a mental environment of ontological conceptions, no matter whether those of everyday life or the most advanced scientific theories, the situation we have indicated remains fundamental for society. We can see this at work in social being, and inevitably so, from the *'asebeia'* trials in Athens, via Galileo and Darwin, through to relativity theory. The dialectical character of labour as a model for social practice shows itself precisely in the way that this social practice in its more developed forms exhibits many departures from labour itself. We have already described above a further form of these mediated complications, and one that is linked in many ways with that now under discussion. Both analyses show that labour is the underlying and hence the simplest and most elementary form of those complexes whose dynamic interaction is what constitutes the specificity of social practice. Precisely for this very reason, it is necessary time and again to point out that the specific features of labour should not be transposed directly to the more complicated forms of social practice. The identity of identity and non-identity in its structural forms, which we have repeatedly indicated, is reducible, we believe, to the way that labour itself materially realizes the radically new relationship of metabolism with nature, whereas the overwhelming majority of other more complicated forms of social practice already have this metabolism with nature, the basis of man's reproduction in society, as their insuperable precondition. Only in the following chapters will we be able to deal with these more complicated forms, and in a really adequate manner only in our Ethics.

But before we pass on to a presentation of the relationship of theory and practice (and, it should be stressed again, simply a preliminary and introductory one), it would appear useful to cast a further glance back to the ontological conditions of the rise of labour itself. In inorganic nature there is simply no such thing. And what gives rise to the appearance of labour in organic nature depends essentially on the way that the reproduction process in organic nature, at its most developed levels, involves interactions between organism and environment which are directly governed by a consciousness. But even at these higher levels (we are referring to animals living in freedom), these are merely biological reactions to those phenomena in the environment that are important for immediate existence, and they cannot therefore give rise to any kind of relationship between subject and object. What this requires is that kind of distancing that we have already described. The object can only become the object of consciousness when consciousness seeks to grasp it even in those respects in which no immediate biological interests link the organism conducting the movements with the object. On the other hand, the subject only becomes a subject by an appropriate transformation in his attitude to the objects of the external world. From this we can see that the positing of the teleological goal and the causally functioning means of its realization cannot be carried out as separate and unrelated acts of consciousness. The inseparable interweaving of teleology and posited causality that we have established is reflected and realized in this complex of executed labour.

This original structure of labour, as we could call it, has its correlative in the way that the realization of the posited causal series provides the criterion for whether its positing has been correct or defective. It is clear, therefore, that in labour taken by itself, practice provides the unconditioned criterion for theory. However indubitable this may be in general, and moreover not only for labour in the narrower sense, but also for all those similar activities of a more complicated kind in which human practice also exclusively confronts nature (we may consider, for example, experiment in the natural sciences), it needs to be made far more concrete as soon as the activity in question goes beyond the narrow material basis that characterizes labour (and also the isolated experiment), i.e., as soon as the theoretically posited causality of a concrete complex is to be introduced into the overall context of reality, into its being-in-itself as reproduced in thought. This already happens in the scientific experiment, abstracting at first from its theoretical evaluation. Every experiment is conducted in the interest of a generalization. It sets in motion by teleology a grouping of materials, forces, etc., from whose particular interactions—as undisturbed as possible by heterogenous circumstances, i.e., such as are accidental in relation to the interrelationships sought—it is to be established whether a hypothetically posited causal relationship does in fact correspond to reality, and thus whether this can be taken as valid for future practice. It is clear in this connection that the criteria that held for labour itself remain valid, and indeed immediately assume a still purer form. Experiment can establish just as clear a judgement between true and false as labour itself, and it does so at a higher level of generalization, at which the quantitative relationships involved in this complex of phenomena can be formulated mathematically. Now if the result of the experiment is to be used to improve the labour process, there is nothing problematic about practice as a criterion for theory. The question becomes more complicated when the knowledge thus obtained is to be used for the extension of theoretical knowledge itself. For in this case the issue is not simply whether a particular concrete causal connection is suitable for promoting a particular concrete teleological positing in a particular concrete constellation of circumstances, but also involves a general expansion and deepening, etc., of our knowledge of nature in general. In cases such as this, a merely mathematical grasp of the quantitative aspects of a material relationship is no longer sufficient; the phenomenon must rather be comprehended in the real specificity of its material being, and its essence as thus comprehended must be brought into agreement with other modes of being that have already been established scientifically. This immediately means that the mathematical formulation of the experimental result must be supplemented and completed by its physical, chemical or biological, etc., interpretation. And irrespective of the intentions of those involved, this necessarily involves the transition to an ontological interpretation. For any mathematical formula is in this respect ambiguous; Einstein's conception of the special theory of relativity and the so-called Lorentz transformations are equivalent to one another mathematically, but the debate as to which is correct involves a debate as to the overall picture of the physical world, and thus necessarily spills over into ontology.

This simple truth, however, describes a permanent field of struggle in the history of science. Again, no matter the extent to which this is conscious, all men's ontological conceptions are to a large extent socially influenced, irrespective of whether the component of everyday life, religious belief, etc., is dominant in this. These ideas play an extremely influential role in men's social practice, and often actually congeal into a social power; we may recall Marx's references to Moloch in his doctoral dissertation.[2] This sometimes gives rise to open struggle between ontological conceptions that have an objective scientific basis and those that are simply anchored in social being. In certain circumstances this opposition actually affects the methods of the sciences themselves, and this is characteristic of our own time. The possibility arises that the newly recognized relationships can be practically exploited even if their ontological implications are ignored. This was already recognized quite clearly by Cardinal Bellarmini in Galileo's time, with regard to Copernican astronomy and its opposition to the theological ontology. In modern positivism, Duhem openly championed Bellarmini's view as 'scientifically superior',[3] and it was in the same sense that Poincaré formulated his own interpretation of the methodological essence of Copernicus's discovery: 'It is convenient to assume that the earth rotates, as in this way the laws of astronomy can be expressed in a far simpler language.'[4] This tendency received its most developed form in the classical texts of neopositivism, with any reference to being in the ontological sense being rejected as 'metaphysics', and hence unscientific, and increased practical applicability being taken as the sole criterion for scientific truth.

The ontological antithesis contained in every labour process and the consciousness directing it, i.e., that between genuine knowledge of being by the further scientific development of causal positing on the one hand, and restriction to the merely practical manipulation of concretely recognized causal connections on the other, thus obtains a form that is deeply anchored in our present social being today. For it would be highly superficial simply to attribute this type of solution of the contradiction of practice as the criterion for theory that appears in labour simply to epistemological, formal-logical or methodological views. Questions and answers of this kind never had such a character. It is true that for a long while the undeveloped state of natural knowledge, the limited control of nature, played a major role in making the practice criterion appear in limited or distorted forms of a false consciousness. The concrete forms of this, however, and in particular its influence, extension, power, etc., have always been determined by social relations, naturally in interaction with the narrow ontological horizon. Today, when the material level of development of the sciences would objectively facilitate a correct ontology, this false ontological consciousness in the realm of science, and its intellectual influence, are far more clearly rooted in the prevailing social needs. To take only the most important of these, manipulation in the economy has become a decisive factor for the reproduction of present-day capitalism, and proceeding from this centre it has spread to all areas of social practice. This tendency receives a further support—open or latent—from the religious side. What

Bellarmini was concerned to prevent, some centuries ago, i.e., the collapse of the ontological foundations of religion, has now quite generally come to pass. The ontological dogmas of the religions, as propounded by theology, have been ever more broken down and evaporated, and in their place we have a religious need that proceeds from the nature of contemporary capitalism and whose foundation in consciousness is mainly a subjective one. The methods of manipulation in the sciences make a large contribution to this underpinning, by destroying the critical sense for real being and thus leaving the way clear for a residual* subjective religious need, as well as by the way that certain theories of the contemporary sciences influenced by neopositivism, theories about space and time, the cosmos, etc., facilitate a reconciliation with the fading ontological categories of the religions. It is typical that, while the general position of leading natural scientists here is a superior scientific neutrality of a positivistic hue, there are actually scientists of some repute, with achievements to their credit, who explicitly seek to reconcile such interpretations of the most recent natural sciences with modern religious needs.

In the preceding discussions, we have repeated a point already mentioned earlier. We did so in order to show quite concretely what was previously simply indicated, i.e., that the direct, absolute and uncritical explanation of practice as the criterion for theory is not something unproblematic. However surely this criterion can be applied in labour itself, and to some extent also in scientific experiment, in any more complicated case conscious ontological criticism must intervene if the fundamentally correct property of this criterion function of practice is not to be endangered. We have seen, for instance, and will refer to this again later, how both in the 'intentio recta' of everyday life and in that of science and philosophy, social development can create situations and orientations that deflect this 'intentio recta' and divert it from grasping the reality of being. The ontological criticism that thereby becomes necessary must therefore be unfailingly a concrete criticism, based in the social totality of the time and oriented towards it. It would be extremely erroneous to assume that in all cases science could appropriately correct everyday thought and philosophy the sciences, or that conversely everyday thought could play for science and philosophy the role of Molière's cook. The intellectual consequences of uneven development in society are so strong and so manifold that approaching this complex of problems with a schema of this kind could only lead to further departures from being. Ontological criticism, therefore, must be oriented to the differentiated totality of society—differentiated concretely by class—and to the mutual relationships in the types of behaviour that thus arise. Only in this way can the function of practice, which is of decisive importance for all intellectual development, and for all social practice, be correctly applied as a criterion for theory.

Up till now we have considered the rise of new complexes of new categories, or of categories with a new function (posited causality), predominantly from the side of the objective labour process. It is also necessary, however, to investigate equally the ontological transformations produced by this leap of man's from the sphere of biological being to that of social, in the behaviour of the subject himself. In this connection too, we must start from the ontological co-presence of teleology and posited causality, for the novelty that arises in the subject is a necessary result of this constellation of categories. If we proceed now from the fact that the decisive act of the subject is his teleological positing and the realization of this, it is immediately illuminating that the categorically decisive moment in these acts involves the emergence of a practice determined by the 'ought'. The immediately determining moment of any action intended as a realization must straightaway be the 'ought', since each step in the realization is determined by whether and how it promotes the attainment of the goal. The direction of determination is thereby reversed. The normal causal determinacy of biology, and in man as well as with animals, involves a causal process in which the past inevitably determines the present. Adaptation of the living being to a changed environment takes place with equal causal necessity, since the properties produced in the organism by its past react on such a change to maintain or destroy it. The positing of a goal reverses this relationship, as we have already seen. The goal exists (in consciousness) prior to its realization, and in the process that brings this realization about, each step and each movement is governed by the posited goal (by the future). The meaning of posited causality, from this point of view, is that the causal elements, chains, etc., are selected, set in motion, checked, etc., with the aim of realizing the goal originally decided. Even when, as Hegel put it, nature simply 'works by itself' in the labour process, this is still not a spontaneous causal process, but a teleologically directed one, whose development consists precisely in the improvement, concretizing and differentiation of this teleological direction of spontaneous processes (use of natural forces such as fire and water for the aims of labour). From the point of view of the subject, this behaviour determined by the posited future is precisely a behaviour governed by the 'ought' of the goal.

Here, too, we should guard against projecting categories that can appear only at more developed stages back into this original form. This can only lead, as happened particularly in the case of Kant's philosophy, to a fetishized distortion of the original 'ought', and one which would also have a negative effect on our comprehension of the more developed forms. The fact of the matter, as regards the initial appearance of the 'ought', is simple enough. The positing of causality consists precisely in the recognition of those causal chains and causal relationships which are in a position to realize the posited goal, when appropriately selected, influenced, etc., while the labour process itself is nothing more than this kind of intervention into concrete causal relations in order to bring about the realization of the goal. We have seen how this necessarily gives rise to a continuous chain of alternatives, and how in this connection, the correct decision on each of these is determined by the future, by the goal that is to be realized. This correct knowledge of causality, and its correct positing, can only be comprehended as determined by the goal; observation and application which is extremely purposive in cutting a stone, for example, may spoil the entire labour in grinding it. Correct reflection of reality is of course the insuperable precondition for a correctly functioning 'ought'; but correct reflection can only become effective if it really does promote the realization of what is desired. What is involved here is not simply a correct reflection of reality in general, an adequate reaction to it, but rather that each particular correctness or error, i.e., each particular decision between alternatives in the labour process, can only be judged exclusively by the goal and its realization. Here, too, we are referring to an indelible interaction between the 'ought' and the reflection of reality (between teleology and posited causality), and in this connection we attribute the function of the predominant moment to the imperative. The self-elevation of the earlier forms, the autochtonic character that social being acquires, is precisely expressed in this supremacy of those categories in which the new and more highly developed character of this type of being gains expression as against those on which it is founded.

We have already repeatedly indicated that leaps of this kind from one level of being to a higher one require very long periods of time, and that the development of a mode of being consists in the gradual—contradictory and uneven—acquisition of predominance by its own specific categories. In the ontological history of each of these categories we can see and demonstrate this process of specification. The inability of idealist thinking to comprehend even the simplest and most illuminating ontological relationships has its ultimate methodological basis in the way that it is content with analysing the most highly developed, most spiritualized and subtle forms of appearance of these categories in terms of epistemology or logic, and in this connection does not only just dismiss the complex of problems associated with their real genesis, which is what provides the ontological orientation, but completely ignores it. Only those forms of social practice that are far removed from the metabolism between society and nature are taken into account, and in dealing with these, the often intricate mediations that link them with their original forms are not only not recognized, but oppositions are actually constructed between the original and the developed forms. In this way, the specificity of social being as good as completely disappears in the overwhelming majority of idealistic treatments of these questions; an artificial and rootless sphere of the 'ought' (of value) is constructed and contrasted with man's allegedly purely natural being, even though both are in fact equally social from the ontological point of view. This complex of problems is further confused by the way that vulgar materialism reacts by simply ignoring the role of the 'ought' in social being, and tries to comprehend this whole sphere after the model of pure natural necessity, so that at both extremes—opposed to one another in content and methodology, but actually belonging together—we have a fetishizing of the phenomena.

This fetishizing of the 'ought' is most clearly observable in the case of Kant. The Kantian philosophy investigates human practice only in connection with the highest forms of morality. (The question of how far Kant's erroneous distinction between morality and ethics obscures these discussions 'from above' and leads to their petrification can of course only be dealt with in our own Ethics.) What is to be investigated here is the limits of his views 'from below', as far as the absence of any kind of social genesis is concerned. As in all consistent idealist philosophies, Kant sets up a hypostasizing fetish of reason. In world-views of this kind, necessity loses, even at the epistemological level, the 'if. . . then' character which alone can render it concrete; it simply appears as something absolute. The most extreme form of this absolutizing of reason is naturally enough displayed in morality. The 'ought' is thus torn away from the concrete alternatives facing men—both subjectively and objectively. These appear instead, in the light of this absolutizing of moral reason, simply as adequate or inadequate embodiments of a kind of absolute command-ment, a commandment which therefore remains transcendent towards man himself. As Kant puts it, 'In a practical philosophy, where it is not the reasons of what *happens* that we have to ascertain, but the laws of what *ought to happen,* even although it never does. . .'[5] The imperative that calls forth these 'ought' relationships in man thus becomes a transcendentally absolute (crypto-theological) principle. Its property is based on its presenting 'a rule expressed in an imperative which expresses the objective necessity of action', and related moreover to a being (i.e., man) 'for whom reason is not the sole ground which determines his will'. In this way the real ontological property of human existence, which in fact is not determined solely by the reason that Kant hypostatizes, appears simply as a cosmically (theologically) arising special case for the general validity of the imperative. Kant is very careful to define the objectivity and validity of this imperative for all 'rational beings', as opposed to the social practice of men which is all that we really know. He certainly does not expressly deny that the subjective maxims that arise here to determine behaviour—in contrast to the absolute validity of the imperative—can also operate as a kind of 'ought', but these are no more than 'practical prescriptions', not 'laws', for the reason that 'they lack that necessity which, if it is to be practical, must be independent of pathological conditions, conditions which adhere accidentally to the will'.[6] In this way all concrete properties, attempts, etc., of men are in his view 'pathological', for they coincide only accidentally with this fetishized abstract will. Here is not the place to embark on a detailed criticism of Kant's moral doctrine. All that concerns us here is the ontology of social being and at present the ontological character of the 'ought' in this domain. These few intimations must therefore suffice, though they illuminate Kant's basic position sufficiently for our present purposes. The only other point that should be made, and which similarly brings out the crypto-theological character of this morality, is that Kant was convinced that despite this method of abstracting from all human and social determinations, he could still give an absolute and binding answer to the most mundane moral alternatives. We may recall here the decision of his that is quite well known, as to why one should not embezzle funds deposited, which Hegel already criticized sharply and correctly in his Jena period. Since I have dealt with this criticism in detail in my book on the young Hegel,[7] this reference will be sufficient here.

It is again not accidental that it was precisely Hegel who so resolutely challenged Kant's conception of the 'ought'. True, his own view is also somewhat questionable. Two different tendencies are in direct confrontation in his thinking. On the one hand a just rejection of Kant's transcendental over-extension of the concept of 'ought'. This however leads frequently to a merely abstract and one-sided opposition. This is the case in his *Philosophy of Right,* where Hegel tries to confront directly the internally problematic and ambiguous character of Kant's formal moral sentiment in ethical life. Here Hegel treats the 'ought' exclusively as a form of appearance of morality, as the standpoint 'of ought-to-be, or demand', an activity 'which can never arrive at anything that *is*'. It is only in ethical life, the fulfilled sociality of human existence, that this is attained, and there this Kantian concept of 'ought' therefore loses its meaning and validity.[8] The error of Hegel's position here is connected with the type of polemic he employs. While he criticizes the narrow and confined character of Kant's moral doctrine, he does not manage to surpass this limitation himself. Correct as is his indication of the internally questionable character of Kant's pure morality, his own counterposition of ethical life as fulfilled sociality is off beam, as this ethical life abolishes the 'ought' character of practice in morality.

Where Hegel deals with this complex of questions for himself, and independent of his polemic against Kant, in the *Philosophy of Mind,* he comes much closer to a genuine ontological position, though even here he is still burdened by certain idealist prejudices. In the section on subjective mind, in investigating the practical feeling as one of the stages in its development, he gives the following definition of the 'ought': 'The "Ought" of practical feeling is the claim of its essential autonomy to control some existing mode of fact—which is assumed to be worth nothing save as adapted to that claim.' Here Hegel recognizes quite correctly that the 'ought' is an elementary, initial and original category of human existence. Of course he does not remark here on its relationship to labour, which is somewhat surprising given his basically correct insight into labour's teleological character. And for this reason there follow really idealistic adverse remarks about the relationship of this 'ought' to the pleasant and unpleasant, which he does not refrain from dismissing as 'subjective and superficial' feelings. But this does not prevent him from suspecting that this 'ought' has a definite significance for the whole range of human existence. Thus he says: 'Evil is nothing but the incompatibility between what is and what ought to be', and adds: ' "Ought" is an ambiguous term—indeed infinitely

71

so, considering that casual aims may also come under the form of Ought.'⁹ This extension of the 'ought' concept gains further value by the way that Hegel restricts its validity expressly to human existence (social being), and contests the existence of any kind of 'ought' in nature. Conflicting as these explanations may be, they do show a tremendous step forward from the subjective idealism of his time, and even of a later era. We shall see later on how Hegel sometimes manages to deal with these problems from a still less restricted point of view.

If we are to comprehend correctly what we believe to be the indubitable genesis of the 'ought' in the teleological nature of labour, we must recall once again what we have already explained about labour as a model for all social practice, i.e., that between the model and its later and far more complicated variants there is a relationship of identity and non-identity. The ontological nature of the 'ought' in labour is certainly oriented to the working subject, and determines not only his behaviour in labour, but also his behaviour towards himself as the subject of the labour process. And yet this process, as we have expressly stressed in our discussion, is a process between man and nature, the ontological foundation for the metabolism between man and nature. This property of the goal, the object, and the means also determines the nature of the subject's behaviour; and, moreover, in the sense that from the subject's point of view, too, only a labour that is performed on the basis of the most extensive objectivity can be successful, so that subjectivity in this process must play a role that serves production. It is natural that the properties of the subject (his talent for observation, skill, diligence, endurance, etc.) should influence the course of the labour process to a decisive extent, both extensively and intensively. But all the human abilities that have to be mobilized for this are always essentially directed outward, to the practical mastery and material transformation of the natural object through labour. In so far as the 'ought'

72

also applies to certain aspects of the subject's internal life, and this is unavoidable, its claims are posed in such a way that the internal transformations provide a vehicle for the better control of the metabolism with nature. Man's self-control, which necessarily emerges first of all as the effect of the 'ought' in labour, the growing command of his insight over his own spontaneous biological inclinations, habits, etc., is governed and guided by the objectivity of this process; but this is founded essentially on the natural existence of the object and means, etc., of labour. If we want to understand correctly the aspect of the 'ought' that affects and modifies the subject in labour, then we must proceed from this objectivity as the regulative principle. Its consequence is that the actual behaviour of the worker is decisive for labour in the primary form; and that what happens in the meantime to the subject himself does not necessarily have to exert an influence. We have of course seen how the 'ought' arouses and promotes qualities in labour that later become decisive for more developed forms of practice; it is sufficient here to recall control over the emotions. These transformations in the subject, however, do not involve his totality as a person, at least not directly; they can function excellently in labour itself without interfering with the remaining life of the subject. They certainly contain substantial possibilities for doing so, but only possibilities.

As we have already seen, once the teleological goal becomes that of influencing other people to perform teleological positings in their turn, then the subjectivity of the positer takes on a qualitatively changed role, and the development of human social relations eventually leads to the self-transformation of the subject becoming the direct object of teleological positings of an 'ought' character. These positings, of course, are distinguished not only by their more complicated character, but also qualitatively distinguished, in precisely this way, from those forms of the 'ought' that we have discovered in the labour process. Their detailed analysis belongs to later chapters, and particularly to our Ethics. These undeniable qualitative differences, however, should not obscure the fundamental common situation, i.e., that they are all 'ought' relations, acts in which it is not the past in its spontaneous causality that determines the present, but in which the teleologically posited future task is the determining principle of practice directed towards it.

The old materialism brought the path 'from below' into intellectual disrepute, by seeking to derive the more highly structured and complicated phenomena directly from the lower, as simply the products of these (Moleschott's notorious derivation of thought from the chemistry of the brain, as a purely natural product). The new materialism founded by Marx certainly considers the natural foundation of human existence as insurpassable, but for the new materialism this is simply one more motive for clearly presenting the specifically social character of those categories that arise from the process of the ontological division between nature and society, presenting them in their social character. This is why, in connection with the problem of the 'ought' in labour, labour's function as the realization of the metabolism between nature and society is so important. This relationship is the foundation of both the rise of the 'ought' in general, from the human and social type of need satisfaction, and of its specificity, its special quality and its being-determining limits, which are called into existence and determined by this 'ought' as the form and expression of real relations. Knowledge of this coincidence of identity and non-identity however is not enough for a full understanding of the position. It would be as misguided to attempt to derive the more complicated forms of the 'ought' from the 'ought' in the labour process, by logic for example, as the dualism of their opposition is false in idealistic philosophy. As we have seen, the 'ought' in the labour process already contains possibilities of the most diverse kind, both objective and subjective. Which of these become social realities, and how, depends on the concrete development of society at the time, and as we also know, the concrete determinations of this development can only be understood after the event.

The problem of value is inseparably linked with the problem of the 'ought' as a category of social being. For just as the 'ought' can only play this specifically determining role in the labour process as a determining factor of subjective practice because the goal aimed at is valuable for man, so value cannot be realized in a process of this kind if it is not in a position to posit the 'ought' of its realization to the worker as the guiding thread of his practice. Despite this intimate correlation, which at first glance operates almost as an identity, value still requires a separate treatment. The two categories certainly belong so intimately together because they are both moments of a common complex. But because value influences above all the positing of the goal and is the principle of judgement on the realized product, while the 'ought' rather provides the regulator of the process itself, much must distinguish the two as categories of social being; this does not remove their correlation, but on the contrary makes it more concrete. If we proceed from the fact that it is value that characterizes the end product of the labour in question as valuable or valueless, the question is immediately raised as to whether this characteristic is an objective one or something merely subjective. Is value the objective property of a thing, which is simply recognized by the subject—correctly or otherwise—in the valuing act, or does value arise precisely as the result of valuing acts of this kind?

It is certainly true that value cannot be obtained directly from the naturally given properties of an object. This immediately casts light on all higher forms of value. We do not have to think in this connection of such 'spiritualized' values as the aesthetic or ethical; right at the start of man's economic intercourse Marx establishes, as we showed, the non-natural character of exchange-value: 'So far no chemist has ever discovered exchange-value either in a pearl or a diamond.'[10] At the moment, of course, we are still dealing only with a more elementary form of appearance of value, with use-value, and here we have an indelible tie to natural existence. Something becomes a use-value because it is useful for human life. Since what is involved here is the transition from merely natural being to social, marginal cases are possible, as Marx shows, where a use-value is present without being the product of labour. 'This is the case', says Marx, 'whenever its utility to man is not mediated through labour. Air, virgin soil, natural meadows, unplanted forests, etc., fall into this category.'[11] If we leave aside air, which genuinely does represent a marginal case, then all other objects are valuable as foundations for later useful labour, as possibilities for the creation of products of labour. (We have already indicated earlier that we see the gathering of natural products as already an initial form of labour; a precise survey of its specific features immediately shows that all objective and subjective categories of labour can be seen embryonically in gathering.) Thus it is no departure from the truth, in such a general consideration as this, to see use-values, goods, as concrete products of labour. This has the result that use-value is an objective social form of objectivity. Its social character is founded in labour. The overwhelming majority of use-values have been brought into being by labour, by the transformation of objects, conditions, the effectiveness, etc., of natural objects, and this process develops both in breadth and depth, as a retreat of the natural boundary, with the ever growing development of labour and its increasing social character. (Today even air can have an exchange-value, with the development of hotels, sanatoria, etc.)

Use-values, goods, thus represent a social form of objectivity which is distinguished from the other categories of economics only by the way that, as the objectification of the society's metabolism with nature, it is a characteristic of all social formations and economic systems, and so—at this general level—is not subject to any kind of historical transformation. Of course, its concrete forms of appearance change continually, even within the same formation. Secondly, use-value is something objective within this context. Quite apart from the fact that as social life develops labour steadily increases the number of those use-values that only indirectly serve the satisfaction of needs—we should not forget that if a capitalist buys a machine, for example, it is its use-value he wants to exploit— the utility that makes an object into a use-value can be established with considerable precision even in the earliest period of labour. It does not abolish this utility that it has a teleological character, and its utility for a definite concrete purpose. Thus the use-value does not arise as a mere result of subjective acts of judgement, but these simply make conscious the use-value's objective utility; their rightness or wrongness is established by the objective properties of the use-values, and not vice versa.

Utility as a property of things might seem at first sight paradoxical. Nature knows nothing of such a category, but simply the causally conditioned process of continual change. It is only in the theodicies that such absurd determinations could arise as, for example, made the hare 'useful' as food for the fox. For utility can only define the mode of being of an object with reference to a teleological positing, it is only in this relationship that it pertains to its nature as an existence to be useful or the opposite. In philosophy, therefore, not only did the ontological role of labour have to be comprehended, but also its function in the constitution of social being as a new and autonomous form, before the question could be posed in a way appropriate to the reality. It is easy to understand from a methodological standpoint, therefore, that those who sought to depict the world proceeding from the supposedly teleological character of reality as a whole, attributed the characteristics of objects in nature and society to their creation by the transcendental creator of the world, and sought to found his objectivity on this. As St Augustine said about things: 'A being they have, because they are from thee: and yet no being, because what thou art, they are not. For that truly hath a being, which remains unchangeably.' Thus the being of the thing expresses its value character as God's creation, while the fact that it perishes indicates its non-existent aspects. In this sense, 'all things are good which thou hast made'; 'whenever they shall be deprived of all their goodness, they shall also lose their being'.[12] Of course, this is only a special case of this cosmic and theological foundation of the objectivity of things, and in this way of values. Here we cannot go into any detail as to the very different variants of such positions, but simply establish that here too, objectivity is derived from labour, even if from the transcendental hypostatization of labour in divine creation. But it still follows from this that on the one hand, and still more pronouncedly than is general for idealist views of the world, the most complicated and spiritualized values come into a more or less sharp opposition with material and earthly ones, and it depends on the way that they are posited whether the latter are simply subordinated to them, or, as in the ascetic manner, even rejected. In our Ethics we shall see how behind all value judgements of this kind there are real contradictions of social being; though we cannot yet deal here with the details of this complex of problems.

Yet for all that we do have here an objectivistic response to the problems of value and the good, even if in a transcendentally distorted sense. And because of this transcendental and theological foundation, it is easy to understand how the anti-religious world view that grew up in opposition to this with the Renaissance should have emphasized the subjective acts of valuation. As Hobbes put it: 'But whatsoever is the object of any man's appetite or desire, that is it which he for his part calleth *good:* and the object if his hate and aversion, *evil;* and of his contempt, *vile* and *inconsiderable.* For these words of good, evil, and contemptible, are ever used with relation to the person that useth them: there being nothing simply and absolutely so; nor any common rule of good and evil, to be taken from the nature of the objects themselves; but from the person of the man. . ."[13]

Spinoza expressed himself in very similar terms: 'As for the terms *good* and *bad,* they indicate no positive quality in things regarded in themselves. . . Thus one and the same thing can be at the same time good, bad, and indifferent.'[14]

These important opposition movements against teleological transcendence in the idea of value reach their philosophical summit with the Enlightenment; with the Physiocrats and the English economists of the eighteenth century we find the first attempts to give them an economic foundation. This was given its most consistent form by Bentham, but also its most superficial and lifeless form.[15]

It is particularly instructive for our ontological problem to consider these two extremes, since in both of them socially real systems of values are condemned as valueless or unimportant, in order to find an aboriginal validation of value in values that are either refinedly spiritual, or immediately material. It does not alter this state of affairs that the values that are rejected at the same level have differing contents (e.g., Manichaeism by Augustine). For what results in both cases is denial of the ultimately unitary character of value as a real factor of social being, irrespective of the very major qualitative changes of structure that it undergoes in the course of social development. Only the dialectical method can provide the *tertium datur* to these two extremes. For this alone makes it possible to explain how the decisive categories of a new mode of being are already contained in its ontological genesis—which is why its rise means a leap in development; but also why these are initially present only implicitly *(an sich),* and the development from the implicit to the explicit *(für sich)* must always be prolonged, uneven and contradictory historical process. This superseding of the implicit by its transformation into an explicit involves the most complex determinations of negation, preservation and raising to a higher level, which seem incompatible with one another from the standpoint of formal logic. It is necessary therefore, even in comparing the primitive and the developed forms of value, to bear in mind this complex character of the supersession. The Enlightenment went astray in attempting to derive even the highest virtues from mere utility—which it often did in a sophistic manner, and as often by the sweat of its brow, to give it its due. This direct approach is impossible. But that does not mean that the dialectical principle of preservation has no role to play. Hegel, even though he often fell victim to idealist preconceptions, as we have seen, made the attempt in his *Phenomenology of Mind* to make the objectively existing contradictions of the Enlightenment conception of utility as the fundamental value into the conscious basis of his own dialectical doctrine of contradiction. He never completely lost sight of this sound ontological tendency. Thus in his *History of Philosophy,* for example, he comes to speak of the Stoics' treatment of utility, and shows by careful criticism how false is the 'high-minded' rejection of this category by idealism, as it can and must be preserved even in the higher value-forms of practice, as a superseded moment. This is what Hegel says here: 'Morality does not require to look so coldly on what concerns utility, for every good action is in fact useful, i.e., it has actuality and brings forth something good. An action which is good without being useful is no action and has no actuality. That which in itself is useless in the good is its abstraction as being a non-reality. Men not only may, but must have the consciousness of utility; for it is true that it is useful to know the good. Utility means nothing else but that men have a consciousness respecting their actions.'[16]

In connection with the ontological genesis of value, therefore, we must proceed from the starting-point that labour as the production of use-values (goods) poses the alternative of useful or non-useful for the satisfaction of needs as a problem of utility, as an active element of social being. In tackling the question of the objectivity of value, therefore, it can immediately be seen that this involves an affirmation of the correct teleological positing, or better: The correctness of the teleological positing—assuming correct realization—means a concrete realization of the value in question in its given context. This concreteness in the value relationship must be especially emphasized. For one element of the idealist fetishizing of values is its abstract over-extension of their objectivity, along the same lines as the over-extension of reason with which we have already become familiar. With value, too, therefore, we must stress its 'if. . . then' character in social ontology; i.e., a knife is valuable if it can cut well, etc. The general rule that the object produced is valuable only in so far as it can serve the satisfaction of needs correctly, and in the most optimal way, avoids erecting this 'if. . . then' structure into an abstractly absolute sphere, conceiving instead relation in an abstraction governed by lawful regularity. In this sense the value appearing in labour as a process reproducing use-value is unquestionably objective. Not only because the product can be measured against the teleological positing, but also because this teleological positing itself, in its 'if. . . then' relation to the satisfaction of needs, can be demonstrated and examined as objectively present and at work. Thus there is no question here of valuations as individual positings constituting value as such. On the contrary. The value that appears in the process and endows it with social objectivity is what decides whether the alternative in the teleological positing and its realization was adequate to the value, i.e., correct and valuable.

Here too, of course, as previously with the 'ought', we have made the overall situation far more simple and unambiguous than it is in the more complicated forms, which no longer belong simply to the sphere of society's metabolism with nature, but while always presupposing this sphere as a basis, work themselves out in a world that has become social. This complex of questions, too, can only be treated adequately at a later point. We shall just choose one example in order to indicate methodologically the manner and direction of the newly arising mediations and realizations. Let us take the simplest form of what Marx calls the 'metamorphosis of commodities', i.e., their simple purchase and sale. In order for any commodity exchange to be possible on the basis of exchange-value and money, there must be a social division of labour. But as Marx puts it, 'The social division of labour makes the nature of his labour [the commodity-owner's: G.L.] as one-sided as his needs are many-sided.' This elementary and contradictory consequence of the division of labour brings about a situation in which the acts of purchase and sale, which materially belong together, become divorced and separate from one another in practice, so that they confront one another purely by accident, and 'no one directly needs to purchase because he has just sold', says Marx. We thus see that: 'To say that these mutually independent and anti-thetical processes form an internal unity is to say also that their internal unity moves forward through external antithesis.' Marx points out in the same passage that: 'These forms there-fore imply the possibility of crises, though no more than the possibility.' (The reality of crises requires 'a whole series of conditions. . . which do not yet even exist from the stand-point of the simple circulation of commodities'.)[17]

We need only to mention these few but important elements to see how much more complicated is the real economic process, forever becoming more social, than simple labour, the direct production of use-values. But this in no way excludes the values here arising from having the same objective character. Even the most complicated economy is a resultant of individual teleological positings and their realizations, both in the form of alternatives. To be sure, the overall movement of those causal chains that they call into being gives rise, by their immediate and mediate interactions, to a social movement whose ultimate determinations together comprise a totality in process. And this can no longer be so directly grasped, by the positing individual economic subjects who decide between alternatives, that they could orient their decisions to the world around them with the same complete certainty as was the case with the simple labour that created use-values. In most cases, indeed, man can scarcely follow correctly the consequences of their own decisions. How therefore could their positings of value constitute economic value? But value itself is still objectively present, and its very objectivity also determines—even if without complete certainty on the objective side, or adequate awareness on the subjective—the individual teleological positings that are oriented by value.

We have already partly shown in our chapter on Marx how the social division of labour that becomes ever more complex gives rise to values, and we shall return to this point several times in what follows. Here we simply want to indicate that the division of labour mediated and brought about by exchange-value produces the principle of control of time by a better subjective use of it. As Marx puts it: 'Economy of time, to this all economy ultimately reduces itself. Society likewise has to distribute its time in a purposeful way, in order to achieve a production adequate to its overall needs; just as the individual has to distribute his time correctly in order to achieve knowledge in proper proportions or in order to satisfy the various demands on his activity. Thus, economy of time, along with the planned distribution of labour time among the various branches of production, remains the first economic law on the basis of communal production.'[18]

Marx speaks of this here as the law of social production. And rightly so, for the causal effects of the different phenomena involved combine together to give such a law, reacting thus on the individual acts as a decisive factor, so that individuals must adapt themselves to this law or perish.

Economy of time, however, immediately involves a relation of value. Even simple labour, oriented just to use-value, was a subjugation of nature by and for man, both in its transformation to suit his needs and in his attaining control over his own merely natural instincts and emotions, and is thus a mediating factor in the initial elaboration of his specifically human abilities. The objective orientation of economic law to the saving of time immediately gives rise to whatever is the optimal social division of labour at the time, thus bringing about the rise of a social being at a higher level of a sociality that becomes ever more pure. This movement is thus an objective one, independent of how those involved might conceive it, a step towards the realization of social categories from their initial implicit being into an explicit being that is ever more richly determined and effective. The adequate embodiment of this explicit being-for-itself of the developed sociality that has reached its point of arrival is man himself. Not the abstract idol of an isolated man, which never exists anywhere, but rather man in his concrete social practice, man who embodies and makes a reality of the human race with his acts and in his acts. Marx saw clearly this connection between economics and that which economic life produces in man himself. In a passage which directly links up in its ideas with that previously quoted on economy of time as the value principle of economic life, he writes: 'Real economy. . . consists of the saving of labour time. . . but this saving is identical with development of the productive force. Hence in no way *abstinence from consumption,* but rather the development of power, of capabilities of production, and hence both of the capabilities as well as the means of consumption. The capability to consume is a condition of consumption, hence its primary means, and this capability is the development of an individual potential, a force of production. The saving of labour time [is] equal to an increase of free time, i.e., time for the full development of the individual, which in turn reacts back upon the productive power of labour as itself the greatest productive power.'[19]

Only in our final chapter will we be able to deal in detail with the concrete problems Marx is referring to here, particularly the relationship of leisure to the productivity of labour.

What is of first importance for Marx himself in this passage is not the individual problems that emerge but rather the generally necessary and inseparable connection between objective economic development and the development of man. Economic practice is carried on by men, in their decisions between alternatives, but its totality forms an objectively dynamic complex whose laws run beyond the will of any individual man, confronting him as his objective social reality with all the stubbornness that characterizes reality. Yet in the objective dialectic of this process, these laws produce and reproduce social man at an ever higher level, or to put it more precisely, they produce and reproduce both those relations that make possible man's higher development, and those capabilities in man himself that transform these possibilities into reality. Marx can therefore continue the passage we have just quoted as follows:

'When we consider bourgeois society in the long view as a whole, then the final result of the process of social production always appears as the society itself, i.e., the human being itself in its social relations. Everything that has a fixed form, such as the product, etc., appears as merely a moment, a vanishing moment, in this movement. The direct production process itself here appears only as a moment. The conditions and objectifications of the process are themselves equally moments of it, and its only subjects are the individuals, but individuals in mutual relationships, which they equally reproduce and produce anew. The constant process of their own movement, in which they renew themselves even as they renew the world of wealth they create.'[20]

It is interesting to compare this depiction with that of Hegel which we quoted previously, and in which Hegel stresses the instruments of labour as the objectively enduring moment in labour, in opposition to the transient character of the momentary need whose satisfaction they make possible. Yet the opposition between the two expressions that strikes one at first sight is only an apparent one. Hegel, in analysing the act of labour itself, stressed the tool as a moment that is of lasting effect for social development, a mediating category of decisive importance, as the result of which the individual act of labour goes beyond its individuality and is itself erected into a moment of social continuity. Hegel thus provides a first indication of how the act of labour can become a moment of social reproduction. Marx, on the other hand, considers the economic process in its developed and dynamic totality, and in this totality man must appear as both beginning and end, as initiator and as end-product of the overall process; even if he often seems to vanish in the streams of this process, and in his individual character always does vanish, yet despite this appearance, which of course also has its own foundation, he still composes the real essence of the process.

The objectivity of economic value is founded in the nature of labour as a metabolism between society and man, but the objective reality of its value character points far beyond this elementary connection. Even the most primitive form of labour which posits utility as the value of its product, and is directly related to the satisfaction of needs, sets a process in motion in the man who performs it, the objective intention of which—irrespective of the extent to which this is adequately conceived—leads to the real unfolding of man's higher development. Economic value thus involves a qualitative advance as against that value that was already immanently given with the simple activity of producing use-values. In this connection, a dual and contradictory movement arises. On the one hand the utility character of value takes a step up into something universal, into the mastery of the whole of human life, and this simultaneously with this utility becoming ever more abstract, since an exchange-value that is always mediated and raised to universality, being contradictory in itself, assumes the leading role in human social intercourse. It should not of course be forgotten in this connection that exchange-value can only come to prevail by being based on use-value. The new phenomenon is therefore a contradictory and dialectical development of original determinations that were already present at the beginning, and never simply their simple abstract negation. On the other hand, this development itself, which has led to the creation of such actual social formations as capitalism and socialism, is intrinsically contradictory, in a most important and fruitful way. The developed social character of production gives rise to a closed system of the economic, with its own immanent basis, in which real practice is possible only through an orientation to immanently economic goals and the search for means to achieve them. The rise of the term 'economic man' is by no means accidental, nor simply a misunderstanding; it expresses very adequately and concretely man's immediately necessary behaviour in a world where production has become social. Only his immediate behaviour, of course. For as we had to establish in the chapter on Marx, and must maintain also in our present discussions, there can be no economic acts—from rudimentary labour right through to purely social production—which do not have underlying them an ontologically immanent intention towards the humanization of man in the broadest sense, i.e., from his genesis through all his development. This ontological characteristic of the economic sphere casts light on its relationship with the other realms of human practice. The ontologically primary and founding function thus falls to the economic, as we have repeatedly seen in other contexts. And even though this has already been often explained, it is not superfluous, we feel, to stress here once again that this ontological priority does not involve any kind of hierarchy of values. It only emphasizes the simple fact of existence that one particular form of being forms the indispensable onto-logical foundation for the other, and not vice versa or reciprocally. This contention is in itself completely value-free. Only in theology and theologically tinged idealism does ontological priority simultaneously represent a higher measure of value.

This basic ontological conception also provides the direction and method for conceiving the development within one sphere of being of higher (more complex and further mediated) categories from the simpler that are their genetic basis, both theoretically and in a practical sense. What should be rejected on the one hand is any kind of 'logical deduction' of the construction and arrangement of categories (in this case: of values) that proceeds from their abstractly conceived general concept. For in this way connections and properties whose ontological specificity is actually based in their socio-historical genesis receive the appearance of a systematic conceptual hierarchy, a discrepancy between true being and the supposedly determining concept which can only falsify their concrete nature and interaction. Equally to be rejected, however, is the vulgar materialist ontology that conceives the more complex categories simply as mechanical products of the elementary ones that are their basis, hence both barring the way to any understanding of their particular character, and creating between them a false ostensibly ontological hierarchy, according to which only the elementary categories would have a genuine being. Rejection of both kinds of false

88

conception is particularly important, if we are to grasp correctly the relation in which economic value stands to other values of social practice (as well as to the theoretical behaviour that is most closely linked with these). We have already seen how value is inseparably bound up with the alternative character of social practice. No values are known in nature, but only causal connections and the transformations and changes in things and complexes that these bring about. The effective role of value in the real world is thus confined to social being. We have shown how alternatives in labour and in economic practice are oriented to values that are in no way mere results and summaries, etc., of individual subjective values, but on the contrary themselves decide, in the context of social being, as to the correctness or otherwise of value-directed alternative positings.

In our earlier discussions we already indicated how the decisive distinction between the original alternatives in labour oriented simply to use-value and those at higher levels is based above all in that the former involve teleological positings that transform nature itself, while in the latter the goal in the first place is to influence the consciousness of other people so as to bring about the desired teleological positings on their part. The realm of the socially developed economy involves value positings of both kinds in manifold connections, and even the first kind are subjected to varying alterations in a complex such as this, without losing their original nature. A greater complexity of value and value positings thus arises already in the realm of the economy. But if we now pass to the non-economic realm, then we are faced with still bigger questions, of a qualitatively different order. This in no way means that the continuity of social being ceases; it is still constantly effective. It is clear on the one hand that certain kinds of social practice, and certain rules, which acquire a position of autonomy in the course of history, are by their actual nature simply forms of mediation, and originally came into existence so as better to govern the social reproduction. We can refer here to the sphere of law in the broadest sense of the term *(Recht)*. We have seen however that this mediating function must receive a constitution independent from the economy, and heterogenously structured in relation to it, precisely in order to fulfil its task in the optimal way.* We can see here once again how the real problem is necessarily overlooked both by the idealist fetishizing that would make the sphere of law into something with a basis entirely its own, and by vulgar materialism that would derive this complex mechanically from the economic structure. It is precisely the objective social independence of the realm of law from the economy, combined with the ensuing heterogeneity, that in their dialectical simultaneity determine both the specificity of value and its social objectivity. On the other hand, we have seen both in the Marx chapter and again here that purely economic positings cannot be carried through without awakening and developing human capabilities, in individual men, in their relations with one another, right through to the real formation of the human species (even if in certain circumstances only the possibility of these capabilities, in the sense of Aristotle's *dynamis*), which in their consequences go far beyond the purely economic, though they can never leave the ground of social being as idealism imagines. Every utopia has its content and direction determined by the society that gives rise to it; every one of the historical and human anti-theses it puts forward is related to a particular phenomenon in the socio-historical existence of the here and now. There is no human problem that is not ultimately raised and determined at bottom by the real practice of social life.

Antithesis, in this connection, is simply an important moment of correlation. In the chapter on Marx we already discussed in some detail how the broadest results of human development often appear (and by no means accidentally so) in such antithetical forms, and in this way become the source of unavoidable conflicts of value, in the objective social sense. We may recall, for example, the thesis referred to there of the only true and real development of the human species being unique. Precisely because the development that takes place in the economy is not in its totality a teleologically posited one, but consists, despite its foundation in the individual teleological positings of individual men, of causal chains with a spontaneous necessity, the phenomenal forms that are historically present in them, with concrete necessity, may well display the most acute antithesis between objective economic progress (and hence objectively progress for humanity) and its human consequences. (It is possibly superfluous to repeat here that in our view the phenomenal world forms an existing part of social reality.) We encounter this opposition throughout history, from the dissolution of primitive communism through to the present forms of manipulation. It can be observed straight away in this connection that whereas the alternative position towards economic development itself is to a large extent clear, almost after the model of simple labour, in the taking of moral positions towards the results of economics that determine human life, an antagonism of values seems to prevail. The basis for this is that in cases where the economic and social process moves forwards with a clearness that is determined by causal laws, the alternative reactions to it necessarily give rise to a similar direct clearness in values. Balzac, as the most profound historian of capitalist development in France, shows in the behaviour of his Birotteau the attitude of rejection of the capitalist practices of his time, and although the psychological and moral motives behind this are estimable, this rejection remains something negative, as far as value is concerned, whereas the fact that his assistant and clever stepson Popinot is able to solve the same economic problems rightly receives a positive valuation. It is not accidental, and is characteristic of Balzac's clear vision, that in Popinot's later development he paints the humanly and morally shady side of this economic success relentlessly in the negative.

But this clear distinction between economic alternatives and those that are no longer economic but human and moral, cannot be seen nearly so sharply as in the case of that labour which is nothing but a simple metabolism with nature. Such a clarity as is depicted here can only appear if the economic process is objectively effective as a 'second nature', so to speak, and if the content of the alternative for the individual in question is completely or predominantly focused on the economic domain proper. In other cases the contradictory character between the economic process itself and its social and human modes of appearance, a contradiction which is often directly antagonistic, must necessarily gain the upper hand. In ancient Rome, already, Lucanus clearly expressed the dilemma of values that arises in this case: '*Victrix causa diis placuit, sed victa Catoni.*'* We need only recall the character of Don Quixote, in whom this tension between the passionately rejected but objectively progressive necessity of social development, and the just as passionate avowal of the moral integrity of humankind, even in forms that belong decisively to the past, appears concentrated in the same character as the unification of grotesque foolishness and sublime purity of soul. But we are still a long way from the roots of this contradiction. The immanently law-bound character of the economy produces not only these antagonisms between the objective nature of its process and its particular phenomenal forms in human life, but also makes this antagonism into an ontological foundation of the overall development itself, as, for example, primitive communism is replaced by class society with objective necessity, so that class membership and participation in the class struggle profoundly determine the decisions that every member of society makes in his life. This gives rise to a space for phenomena of conflict, as soon as the content of the alternatives goes decisively beyond the metabolism between society and nature. Frequently, in this connection, the alternatives involved in the realization of values even assume the form of irresolvable conflicts of duty, since in these alternatives the conflict is not merely one of recognizing a value as the 'what?' and 'how?' of decision, but rather determines practice as a mutual conflict between concrete and concretely prevailing values. The alternative is governed by a choice between mutually conflicting values. It appears therefore as if our argument might be leading back to Max Weber's tragic and relativistic conception which has already been mentioned, according to which this conflict-laden and irreconcilable pluralism of values forms the basis of human practice in society.

Yet this is only an appearance. Behind it lies not reality itself, but on the one hand a clinging to the immediacy in which phenomena present themselves in the world of appearance, and on the other hand an over-rationalized, logicized and hierarchical system of values. These equally false extremes, when they alone are brought into play, produce either a purely relativistic empiricism or else a rational construction that cannot be adequately applied to reality; when brought alongside they produce the appearance of an impotence of moral reason in the face of reality. Here we cannot concern ourselves with this complex of questions in concrete detail; this will be one of the tasks of our Ethics. Only there will it be possible to differentiate appropriately between values and realizations of value that are very different in their forms of change and self-preservation. At present we can only indicate this process very generally with one example; that of a socially correct decision in a meaningful alternative. All that is required here is to point out quite summarily the main features of the ontological method with which this complex should be approached. In this connection we must proceed from the definition of substantiality which we spoke of already in previous contexts. Recent insights into being have destroyed the static and unchanging conception of substance; yet this does not mean that it can be dispensed with in ontology, simply that its essentially dynamic character should be recognized. Substance is that which in the perpetual changing of things, while itself changing, is able to maintain itself in its continuity. This dynamic self-maintenance, however, is not necessarily bound up with any 'eternity'. Substances can rise and fall without thereby ceasing to be substances for so long as they dynamically maintain their existence within this period of time.

Every genuine value is then an important moment in that fundamental complex of social being that we denote as practice. The being of social being is maintained as substance in the reproduction process; this however is a complex and synthesis of teleological acts which cannot be materially separated from the acceptance or rejection of a value. Thus a value (positive or negative) is involved in any practical positing, which might give the appearance that values themselves were only social syntheses of such acts. What is correct in this is simply that values could not obtain any ontological relevance in society if they did not have to become the objects of such positings. Yet this condition of the realization of value is not simply identical with the ontological genesis of value. The true source of the genesis is rather the continuous structural change in social being itself, from which social being the value-realizing positings directly arise. It is a basic truth of the Marxian conception, as we have already seen, that while men make their own history, they do not make it in circumstances they have themselves been able to choose. Men rather respond—more or less consciously, more or less correctly—to those concrete alternatives that the possibilities of social development place before them at the time. Here, however, value is already implicitly involved. If, for example, man's control of his emotions as the result of labour is a value, as it undoubtedly is, it is contained in labour itself and can become a social reality without necessarily having to immediately have a conscious form and making its value character something actual for the working man. It is a moment of social being, and is therefore really existent and effective even if it is not conscious, or only incompletely so.

Naturally, this coming to consciousness is also not socially accidental. We have had to lay particular stress on this moment of independence in order to properly accentuate the socially ontological character of value. It is a social relation between goal, means and individual, and it is as such that it possesses a social being. Naturally this being also contains an element of possibility, since in itself it only determines the room for manoeuvre between concrete alternatives, their social and individual content, the directions of resolution of the questions they involve. The development of this implicit being-in-itself, its growth into a genuine being-for-self, value attains in the acts that fulfil it. But it is characteristic for the ontological situation we are faced with here that this realization that is indispensable for the ultimate reality of value remains indissolubly linked to value itself. It is value that gives its realization its specific characteristics, and not the other way round. This must not be understood as if the realization of value could be 'derived' from it in thought, or as if the realization were a simple product of human labour. Alternatives are the indelible foundations for specifically human social practice, and only by abstraction, never in reality, can they be divorced from the individual decision. The significance of such alternatives for social being, however, depends on value, or better, on the complex of real possibilities at the time of reacting practically to the problem of a socio-historical here and now. Thus the decisions that realize these real possibilities in their purest form—whether affirmatively or negatively—attain a positive or negative model character appropriate to the level of development of the time.

At a primitive level this is obtained through direct verbal tradition. The mythical heroes are those who responded to the alternatives of tribal life (culminating in values) at such a level of example that this response has come to be of lasting social importance, in an exemplary way (positively or negatively) for the life of the tribe and its reproduction, and has thus become a component part of this reproduction process in both its change and its self-maintenance.

Perpetuation of this kind needs no special demonstration; it is a generally known fact how such personal decisions between alternatives have been retained in memory from the era of myth creation through to the present. Yet the mere retaining of these decisions only expresses one aspect of the process. It is just as important to establish that this only becomes possible if they can always be subjected to a continuous change in interpretation, i.e., in their applicability as an example for practice in the present. The basic situation here is not affected by the fact that in the earliest times this was done by way of oral tradition, later by poetic and artistic characterization, etc. For in all these cases what is involved is that an action oriented to a social alternative is essentially permanently preserved for social being while its concrete details, interpretation, etc., undergo constant change. The specific character of the value being realized here is expressed in the way that the form is one of an individual alternative, and not, as in some other realms of value, that of a commandment or taboo. It arises directly from the human personality, and its self-confirmation shows the inner kernel of the human species in its continuity. The true social context is shown above all by the way that the ultimately decisive moment of change and reinterpretation is always anchored in the social needs of the time. These needs determine whether and how the alternative fixed in this way is interpreted. It is not the discovery of a possible historic truth that is decisive here. We know full well that the Brutus of the legend does not correspond to historic truth; but this does not reduce in the slightest the effect of Shakespeare's character, and opposite valuations (e.g., Dante's) are similarly rooted in the needs of their own time. Change and constancy are thus both produced by social development; their interrelation reflects precisely that newly recognized form of substantiality which we referred to at the start of this train of thought, an organic component of which is value in its historical objectivity.

The objectivity of values thus rests on the way that these are moving and moved components of the overall social development. Their contradictory character, the incontestable fact that they stand very often in express opposition to their economic basis and to one another, is in this way no sign of an ultimate relativism of values, as Max Weber believed, and still less is the impossibility of arranging them in a hierarchic and tabular system. Their existence, which is played out in the form of an 'ought' whose obligatory character is that of a social fact, involving by inherent necessity their plurality, their mutual relationship in a scale leading from heterogeneity to opposition, can only be rationalized after the event, and this precisely expresses the contradictory unity and the uneven clarity of meaning of the overall socio-historic process. This last, in its objective causal determinacy, forms a dynamic totality; but since it is constructed from the causal summation of alternative teleological positings, each moment that directly or indirectly consolidates or inhibits it always consists of such alternative teleological positings. The value of these positings is decided by their true intention, as this becomes objective in practice, and this can be governed by something essential or fleeting, progressive or inhibiting, etc. Since all these tendencies are really present and effective in social being, since they therefore give rise to alternatives for men in their actions that are quite different in direction, level, etc., the appearance of relativity is in no way accidental. This also contributes towards a tendency towards authenticity remaining alive in the questions and answers, or at least partially so, since the alternative of the practice of the time is not only expressed in affirming or rejecting a particular value, but also in which value forms the basis of the concrete alternative and the reasons why such a position is taken towards it. We know that economic development provides the objective backbone of actual progress. The decisive values, therefore, those perpetuating themselves in the process—consciously or unconsciously, directly or possibly in a highly mediated way—always relate to this; but there are objectively important distinctions to be made as to which moments of this overall process the alternative in question envisages and confronts. This is the way values maintain themselves in an overall social process that is continuously repeated, this is the way they become, in their own way, existing components of the social being in its reproduction process, elements of a complex 'social being'.

We have deliberately selected for the purpose of demonstrating this ontological situation a value that is very far removed from labour as a model. We take this first of all so as to show that even in cases of this kind, in which the alternative has directly become already a purely spiritual one, objective conditions of social existence still underly the intention behind the decision, so that the value realized in practice must still have an objective social character. We referred above to the character of Brutus as an example, in which case this connection, this rooting of the value in social being, could be palpably grasped. It is equally visible, and perhaps even more so, if we recall how in the eyes of Hesiod Prometheus was a criminal justly punished by the gods, while from Aeschylus's tragedy onwards his character lives on in human consciousness as the bringer of light and a benefactor. If we add that the Old Testament doctrine of the Fall (with labour as the punishment) and the Christian teaching of original sin both represent the same standpoint as Hesiod with an increased social effectiveness, then it is easy to see that in this case the content of the alternatives was to decide whether man was to bring himself into existence as man by his labour—or whether he was to be conceived as the product and servant of transcendent powers, from which it necessarily follows that every autonomous act that is founded in man himself, in his social being, involves a crime against these higher powers. But in social being's coming to prevail in the alternatives, however—and this is the second point—this structure that it has here is an extreme though highly significant case, and can become operative in human history only at a relatively developed level. The socially necessary positing of values must therefore also produce cases with a different structure. Since this complex of problems can only be adequately dealt with as a whole in our Ethics, we confine ourselves here to some indications that are purely formal in character. There are social values that require an institutional apparatus, which may of course assume very different forms, in order to prevail in society (law, the state, religion, etc.), and there are cases in which the objectifications of the reflection of reality becomes bearers of values, occasions for their positing, etc. The differences and heterogenous structures that give rise to direct antitheses cannot even be indicated here, for these are without exception expressed adequately only in the concrete social interrelations and interactions between values, and can therefore only be grasped in a really synthetic presentation directed towards the totality of social practice and thus of social being.

3. *The Subject-Object Relation in Labour and its Consequences*

We have not yet finished, by a long way, with those forms of appearance of the specifically human way of life which arise from labour and must thus be comprehended ontologically and genetically on this basis, no matter how far-reaching their mediations. But before we can deal in any more detail with questions that are apparently very far removed from this starting-point, no matter how fundamentally they are rooted in it, we must consider somewhat more closely a direct consequence of labour that we have already touched on before, i.e., the rise of the subject-object relation and the really effective and necessary distancing of the object from the subject this involves. This distancing creates both an indispensable basis for human social existence, and one that is endowed with a life of its own: language. Engels is right to say that language arose from men arriving at a point where '*they had something to say* to each other. Necessity created the organ; the undeveloped larynx of the ape was slowly but surely transformed. . .'[1] But what exactly does it mean to have something to say? We already find communications of various kinds in the higher animals, including highly important ones relating to danger, food, sexual desire, etc. The leap between communications such as these and those of men, which Engels so pertinently indicates, consists precisely in this distance between subject and object. Man always speaks 'about' something definite, thereby contrasting it in a double sense with his immediate existence. Firstly, by positing it as an independently existing object, and secondly—and here the distancing process comes even more sharply to the fore—by striving to indicate the object in question as something concrete; his means of expression and his descriptions are constructed in such a way that each sign can equally well figure in completely different contexts. In this way what is depicted by the verbal sign is separated from the objects it describes, and hence also from the subject uttering it, becoming the mental expression for an entire group of particular phenomena, so that it can be applied in a similar way in completely different contexts and by completely different subjects. The forms of animal communication know nothing of this kind of distancing, they form an organic component of the biological life process, and even when they do have a clear content this is bound up with particular concrete situations in which the animals are involved. In this case, therefore, we can only speak of subjects and objects in a very much borrowed sense, one that can easily be misunderstood, even though it is still a concrete living being that is seeking to communicate about a concrete phenomenon, and even though these communications are generally extremely clear in the particular situation to which they are inseparably linked. The simultaneous positing of subject and object in labour, and similarly in the language that arises from it, distances the subject from the object, and vice versa, as well as the concrete object from its concept, etc., in the sense referred to here. This makes possible a comprehension of the object and its mastery by man which is in principle infinitely extendable. It is not surprising that the naming of objects, the uttering of their concept and name, was long taken as magic, as a miracle; even in the Old Testament, the mastery of man over the animals is expressed in Adam giving them their names, something which at the same time clearly indicates the emergence of language from nature.

The creation of this distance, however, is itself ever more differentiated, both in labour and in language. Even the simplest form of labour, as we have seen, realizes a new relationship of immediacy and mediation by its dialectic of end and means, by each satisfaction of needs that is attained through labour being already something mediated by its own objective nature. The equally insuperable fact that every product of labour, when finished, possesses a new and no longer natural immediacy for the man using it, strengthens the antithetical character of this state of affairs. (Boiling or roasting meat is a mediation, but eating boiled or roasted meat is in this sense just as immediate as eating raw meat, even if the latter is natural and the former social.) In its further development, labour constantly interposes whole series of mediations between man and the immediate goal which he is ultimately concerned to achieve. In this way labour gives rise to a differentiation between immediate and more mediated goal positings that already appears even earlier. (We may refer to the production of weapons, which requires the discovery of ore and its smelting and a whole series of different and heterogenous teleological positings before the finished product appears.) Social practice is possible only if this conduct towards reality has become socially general. It goes without saying that an expansion of labour experience of this kind gives rise to completely new relationships and structures, but this cannot alter the fact that this distinction between the immediate and the mediate—given their simultaneous existence in a necessary connection, their succession, super- and subordination, etc.—has arisen from labour. The mental distancing of objects by language only makes the real distancing that thus arises communicable, making possible its establishment as the common possession of a society. We need only think how the temporal succession of different operations, and their mediations according to the nature of the thing in question (sequence, pause, etc.) could not possibly have been carried through on a social scale—just to stress the most important aspect—without a clear division of time in language, etc. Just like labour, language also represents a leap from natural to social being; and in both cases this leap is a lengthy process, so that while its first beginnings will always remain unknown to us, their direction of development can be studied quite precisely with the aid of the development of tools, and can even be surveyed in retrospect to some extent as a whole. Of course the earliest linguistic benchmarks that ethnography is able to provide for us are of much later date than the earliest tools. But a linguistics that would take as its object of research or methodological guide the really existing connections between labour and speech could broaden and deepen our knowledge of the historical process of this leap to an extraordinary extent.

As we have already explained in detail, labour necessarily also changes the nature of the men performing it. The direction taken by this process of transformation is immediately given by the teleological positing and its practical realization. As we have shown, the central question of the internal transformation of man consists in his attaining a conscious control over himself. Not only does the goal exist in consciousness before its material realization; this dynamic structure of labour also extends to each individual movement. Labouring man must plan every moment in advance and permanently check the realization of his plans, critically and consciously, if he is to achieve in his labour the concrete optimal result. This mastery of the human body by consciousness, which also affects a portion of the sphere of consciousness itself, i.e., habits, instincts, emotions, etc., is a basic requirement of even the most primitive labour, and must therefore give a decisive stamp to the ideas that men form of themselves, since it requires a relationship to self that is qualitatively different from the animal constitution, completely heterogenous from this, and since these requirements obtain for every kind of labour.

The new property of human consciousness that we have already described from various aspects, i.e., that it ceases to be a biological epiphenomenon and forms an essential and active moment of the newly arising social being, is an objective ontological fact. If we have depicted in many different ways the retreat of the natural boundary as a result of labour, then this new function of consciousness, as the bearer of the teleological positings of practice, plays an extremely important role in this connection. But in approaching this complex of problems from the strict standpoint of ontological criticism, it is necessary to remember that while there is certainly a permanent retreat of the natural boundary, this can never be completely abolished. Man, as the active member of society, the motor of its changes and forward movements, remains insurpassably a natural being, in the biological sense. In this biological sense his consciousness remains, despite even ontologically decisive changes of function, inseparably linked to the process of biological reproduction of his body; the biological basis of life persists unchanged even in society, in the universal fact of this linkage. All the possibilities there are of prolonging life, for example, by the application of science, cannot alter this ultimate ontological linkage of consciousness to the process of bodily life.

Considered ontologically, this characteristic, the relationship between two spheres of being, is nothing structurally new. Already in biological being, physical and chemical relationships, processes, etc., are insuperably given. If these are able—and the more so, the higher the organism is developed—to perform functions that would be impossible for purely physical or chemical processes that were not tied to the organic, this can in no way abolish the inseparable tie that binds the organism to the basis of its normal functioning. Different as the relationship between social and biological being is from that just mentioned between organic and inorganic, this linkage between the more complex higher system and the existence, reproduction, etc., of that which founds it 'from below' remains an unalterable ontological fact. In itself, this connection will not be contested; yet the development of consciousness creates socially relevant positings that can lead the ontological 'intentio recta' onto false paths even in everyday life. The deviations from these basic facts of ontology that thus arise are already for this reason quite difficult to see through and overcome, since they appear to be based on immediate and insuperable facts of consciousness. If the complexity of this situation is not to be simplified in a vulgarizing way, then the word 'appear' should not be put in brackets; it must rather be constantly borne in mind that what this appearance expresses is a necessary phenomenal form of human social being, which when considered in isolation must thus appear as something irrefutable. Its character, even if that of a mere appearance, can only be brought to light by analysing the concrete complex in its dynamic full of contradictions.

We are thus confronted with two seemingly opposing facts. Firstly the objective ontological fact that the existence and effectiveness of consciousness is inseparably linked with the biological process of the living organism, and that every individual consciousness—and there can be no other kind—arises together with the body in question and perishes with it also. Secondly, the leading, guiding and determining role of consciousness vis-à-vis the body; in the interconnection of the two that is thus given, the body appears as the servant and executive organ of the teleological positings that can only proceed from and be determined by consciousness. This basic fact of social being, about which there cannot be any doubt, i.e., the mastery of consciousness over the body, gives rise in human consciousness, with a certain degree of necessity, to the idea that consciousness or the 'soul' that is thought of as its substantial bearer could not possibly guide and control the body if it were not a substance independent of the body, qualitatively different from it in constitution and possessing an existence of its own. It is evident from any unprejudiced and unconfined treatment of this complex of problems—which of course is quite a rarity—that no matter how certain is the consciousness of this autonomy, this is still no proof of its actual existence. In so far as any kind of existence can have an independent being, and this is always a relative relationship, it must always be possible to derive such independence ontologically and genetically; independent functioning within a complex is not sufficient proof. And the proof that is required relates to man in his totality, as individual and personality (only within social being, of course, and so here too only relatively), and thus never simply to body or consciousness (soul) each considered in isolation; in this connection an indelible unity is given as an objective ontological fact, the impossibility of consciousness existing without the simultaneous existence of the body. Ontologically, it must be said that the body can exist without consciousness, e.g., if consciousness ceases to function as the result of illness, whereas consciousness can have no existence at all without a biological foundation. This in no way contradicts the independent, guiding and planning role of consciousness vis-à-vis the body, but is rather its ontological foundation. The contradiction between appearance and essence is thus present here in an extremely blatant form. It should not be forgotten, of course, that antitheses of this kind between appearance and essence are by no means so uncommon; it is sufficient to consider the movement of the sun and the planets, where the appearance that runs diametrically counter to the essence is so firmly given for the earth's inhabitants in their immediate sensuous reflection of the phenomena that even for the most convinced upholders of the Copernican conception the sun still rises in the morning and sets in the evening, as far as their immediate sensuous everyday life is concerned.

If this latter contradiction between appearance and essence in human consciousness lost its character of a primarily ontological contradiction somewhat more easily, if still only slowly, and could become conscious as what it is, i.e., a contradiction between appearance and essence, this is because what is at issue here is simply the external life of man and does not necessarily affect directly his relationship to himself. This question did of course play a certain role in the breakdown of the religious ontology and the transformation of faith founded on ontology into a purely subjective religious need, though this is something that we cannot go into here in any more detail. As regards the question we are concerned with at the moment, on the other hand, what is involved is the vital interest for every person in his everyday life that his mental picture of himself has. Added to this and reinforcing it is the fact that even though the objective ontological independence of the 'soul' from the body is based simply on an unfounded assumption, an isolating and false abstraction in the view of the overall process, yet the independent actions of consciousness, the specific nature of the teleological positings that proceed from it, the conscious control of their execution, etc., are still objective facts of ontology and of social being. Thus if consciousness conceives its own independence from the body as an ontological absolute, it goes astray not in the immediate mental establishment of the phenomenon, as with the planetary system, but simply in treating the ontologically necessary mode of appearance as founded directly and adequately in the thing itself. The difficulty experienced in overcoming this necessarily dualist mode of appearance of what is ontologically ultimately a unitary complex of forces is to be seen not only in the religions, but also time and again in the history of philosophy. Even those thinkers who were otherwise seriously and successfully concerned to purge philosophy of transcendental and theological dogmas slipped up here and only perpetuated the old dualism in new formulations. It is sufficient to recall the great philosophers of the seventeenth century, among whom this mode of appearance was preserved as an ontological ultimate, in the insurpassable duality between extension and thought (Descartes). Spinoza's pantheism shifted the solution to a transcendental infinity; this is most forcibly expressed in the ambiguity of his *deus sive natura*. And the whole of occasionalism is nothing more than an attempt to reconcile the basic problem intellectually without a real ontological extrication of the confusion. The difficulty faced in seeing through· this erroneous path taken by the ontological *'intentio recta'* in both everyday life and philosophy is increased further in the course of development of social being. Of course the development of biology as a science supplies ever new and better arguments for the inseparability of consciousness and being, the impossibility of a 'soul' existing as an independent substance.

Other forces in social life, however, as this is organized at an ever higher level, operate in the opposite direction. What we have in mind here is the complex of problems which can be described as the meaningfulness of life. This meaning is posed socially, by man for man, for himself and his kind; nature knows nothing of this category, and so neither of the negation of meaning. Life, birth and death as phenomena of natural life are devoid of meaning, being neither meaningful nor meaningless. It is only when man in society seeks a meaning for his life that the failure of this attempt brings in its wake the antithesis of meaninglessness. At the beginnings of society this particular effect still appears simply in a spontaneous and purely social form. A life according to the commands of society at the time is meaningful, e.g., the heroic death of the Spartans who fell at Thermopylae. It is only when society becomes so differentiated that a man can individually shape his life in a meaningful way or else surrender it to meaninglessness that this problem arises as a general one, and with it also a further deepening of the consideration of the 'soul' as independent, now not only expressly from the body, but also vis-à-vis its own spontaneous emotions. The unchangeable facts of life, and above all death, one's own as well as that of others, makes consciousness of this meaningfulness into a socially believed reality. In itself, the striving to make life meaningful by no means necessarily reinforces this dualism between body and soul; we can see this simply by thinking of Epicurus. Yet his case is not the general rule of such developments. The teleology of everyday life spontaneously projected onto the external world, as we have already mentioned, promotes the construction of ontological systems in which the meaningfulness of individual life appears as a part and a moment of a universal teleological work of redemption. Whether it is bliss in heaven that forms the crowning end of the teleological chain, or alternatively dissolution of the self in a blissful non-objectivity, a salvation through non-being, all this is irrelevant to our present discussion. What is important is that the desire to preserve the meaningful integrity of the personality, which from a certain level of development onwards becomes an important problem of social life, receives mental support from a fictitious ontology that is developed from needs of this kind.

We have deliberately brought in such very far-reaching and mediated consequences of the phenomenon we are concerned with here, the false ontological depiction of an elementary fact of human life. For it is only in this way that we can see how broad a field labour gives rise to in the humanization of man, both extensively and intensively. The mastery of all other aspects of man by a consciousness that sets goals, and above all its mastery over his own body, the distanced and critical relationship of human consciousness to the person itself that is thereby attained, can be traced throughout human history, if in constantly changing forms and with new and ever differentiated contents. And the origin of this mastery lies undoubtedly in labour. Analysis of labour leads unforcedly and automatically to this group of phenomena, whereas all other attempts at explanation, even though they are not aware of it, presuppose the self-experience that man acquires in labour. It is erroneous, for example, to seek the origin of this independence of the 'soul' in the experience of dreaming. Some higher animals also dream, without the epiphenomenal character of their animal consciousness being thereby able to take a turn in this direction. Added to this is the fact that the very strangeness of the dream experience consists precisely in the way that its subject, interpreted as the soul, embarks on courses of action that seem more or less incongruent with its normal dominance in life. But once, as a result of the waking experiences of labour, the independent existence of the 'soul' has become a fixed point in man's image of himself, then, but only then, dream experiences can lead to a further mental construction of their transcendental being. This already happens with magic, and with appropriate modifications also in the later religions.

It should not be forgotten, however, that both the mastery of otherwise unmastered natural forces that is aimed at in magic, and the religious conceptions of creator gods, have human labour as their ultimate underlying model. Engels, who occasionally touched on this problem too, though he was more interested in the origin of the philosophical idealist view of the world, seeks to derive it from the fact that even at a relatively low stage of development (in the primitive family), 'the mind that planned the labour was able. . . to have the labour that had been planned carried out by other hands than its own'.[2] This is certainly correct for those societies in which ruling classes have already completely ceased to work themselves, and in which therefore the physical labour that is performed by slaves comes to be viewed with social contempt, as in the developed Greek *polis*. But any contempt in principle for physical labour is still unknown in the heroic world of Homer; here work and leisure have not yet devolved, in the class division of labour, onto different social groups. 'It is not the portrayal of satisfaction that stimulates him [Homer: G.L.] and his listeners, they rather experience pleasure in the actions of man, in his ability to win his daily bread and prepare it, and thus strengthen himself. . . The division of human life into labour and leisure has not yet appeared in its concrete context in the Homeric epic. Man labours; this is necessary in order to eat and in order to conciliate the gods with sacrifices of flesh, and when he has eaten and given sacrifice, then his free enjoyment begins.'[3] When Engels goes on to say, in the passage quoted above, that the ideological process he is referring to 'has dominated men's minds. . . since the fall of the world of antiquity', he is

110

indicating the effect that Christian spiritualism had on their world view; yet Christianity, and particularly in its first beginnings, when its spiritualism possibly was at its height, was in no sense the religion of an upper stratum freed from physical labour. If we stress once again here that it is in labour itself that the objectively effective but ontologically relative independence of consciousness from the body arises, together with its—apparently—complete independence and the reflection of this in the experience of the subject as a 'soul', it is far indeed from our mind to seek to derive later and more complex conceptions of this complex directly from this. What we maintain, on the basis of the ontology of the labour process, is merely the simple state of affairs that we have already described. If this can express itself very differently at different stages of development and in different class conditions, these differentiations of the content of the time, which are often opposed and contrary, arise from the structure of the social formation in question. This of course in no way rules out the foundation of these different and specific phenomena from being precisely that ontological situation which must necessarily arise with and in labour.

The very question as to whether the independence of the 'soul' is presented as an earthly one or as involving a beyond can already not be simply derived from the origin. It is clear enough that most ideas of magic were essentially earthly and this-sided. The unknown natural forces were to be mastered by magic in the same way as the known forces were mastered by normal labour, and magical measures of defence against the possibly dangerous interventions of 'souls' that had become independent through death correspond completely, in their general structure, to the everyday teleological positings of labour, however fantastic they may be in their content. The very demand for a beyond where the meaningfulness of life that is disrupted and remains fragmentary on earth may be somehow fulfilled, whether by salvation or damnation, arose—as a general human phenomenon—from the situation of men in this position, for whom the life open to them could not provide any fulfilment on earth. Max Weber is correct to point to the opposite extreme of how for a class of warriors a beyond sometimes appears 'reprehensible to its sense of honour'. 'It is an everyday psychological event for the warrior to face death and the irrationalities of human destiny. Indeed, the chances and adventures of mundane existence fill his life to such an extent that he does not require of religion (and accepts only reluctantly) anything beyond protection against evil magic or such ceremonial rites as are congruent with his caste, such as priestly prayers for victory or for a blissful death leading directly into the hero's heaven.'[4] It is enough to think of Dante's Farinata degli Uberti, or the Florentines praised by Machiavelli, for whom the salvation of their city was more important than the salvation of their own souls, to see the correctness of this train of thought. Such variety, which is only a small section of that realized in social being, naturally needs to be given a particular explanation in each new historic form. But this does not rule out the fact that none of these forms could become real without that ontological separation between consciousness and body which is given its first and generally prevailing function, that which is fundamental to it and is the basis of everything more complex, in labour. In labour and in it alone, therefore, can we seek and find the ontological genesis of the later and more complex social phenomena.

How fundamental labour is for the humanization of man is also shown in the fact that its ontological constitution forms the genetic point of departure for yet another question of life that has deeply affected men over the entire course of their history, the question of freedom. In considering this question, too, we must apply the same method as before. That is, point out the original structure that forms the point of departure for the later forms, and their insurpassable foundation, while simultaneously bringing to view those qualitative distinctions that appear in the course of the later social development, spontaneously and unavoidably, and which necessarily modify decisively, even in important respects, the original structure of the phenomenon. The particular difficulty for a general methodological investigation of freedom lies precisely in the fact that it belongs to the most manifold, many-sided and scintillating phenomena of social development. We could say in fact that each particular area of social being which has to some extent obtained its own laws produces its own form of freedom, which is also subject to significant changes simultaneously with the social and historical development of the sphere in question. Freedom in the legal sense means something essentially different from the sense of politics, morality, ethics, etc. An adequate treatment of the question of freedom, therefore, can only be given in our Ethics. Yet it is already of the utmost theoretical importance to make this differentiation, since idealist philosophy seeks at all costs to construct a unitary and systematic concept of freedom, sometimes even believing itself to have found such a concept. Here, too, we can see the erroneous consequences of that widespread tendency that attempts to resolve ontological questions with the methods of logic and epistemology. This gives rise on the one hand to a false and often fetishizing homogenization of what are in fact heterogenous complexes of being, while on the other hand, as was already shown before, the more complicated forms are used as models for the simpler, which makes methodologically impossible both the genetic understanding of the former and analysis of the latter by the correct standards.

If, after these indispensable reservations, we now try and explain the ontological genesis of freedom in labour, we must naturally proceed from the alternative character of the positing of goals in labour. In this alternative, in fact, the phenomenon of freedom that is completely foreign to nature appears for the first time in a clearly defined form. Since consciousness decides, in the alternative manner, which goal to posit and how the causal series required for it are to be transformed into posited ones as a means of realization, ther ˙ arises a dynamic complex of reality for which no analogy of any kind can be found in nature. It is only here, therefore, that the phenomenon of freedom can be investigated in its ontological genesis. In a first approximation, we can say that freedom is that act of consciousness which has as its result a new being posited by itself. Here, already, our ontological and genetic conception departs from that of idealism. For in the first place, the basis of freedom, if we want to speak meaningfully of freedom as a moment of reality, consists in a concrete decision between different concrete possibilities. If the question of choice is taken to a higher level of abstraction, then it is completely divorced from the concrete, and thus loses all connection with reality, becoming an empty speculation. In the second place, freedom is ultimately a desire to alter reality (which of course includes in certain circumstances the desire to maintain a given situation), and in this connection reality must be preserved as the goal of change, even in the most far-reaching abstraction. Our former considerations have of course also shown how the intention of a decision that is directed, via mediations, towards changing the consciousness of another person, or one's own; also aims at a change of this kind. The orbit of real goal positings that thereby arises is thus a large one and encompasses a great diversity; but it still has precisely definable limits in each individual case. Thus in as much as no intention of this kind to change reality can be demonstrated, such states of consciousness as deliberations, plans, wishes, etc., have no direct connection with the real problem of freedom.

The question as to how far the external or internal determination of the decision can be conceived as a criterion for freedom is rather more complicated. If the antithesis between determinacy and freedom is conceived in an abstract and logicizing sense, then the end result is that only an all-powerful and all-knowing god could really be inwardly free, though by his theological nature he would then again exist beyond the sphere of freedom. As a determination of men living and acting in society, freedom is never completely free from determination. We need only recall our previous discussions to see that even in the most simple labour certain nodal points of decision appear, such that the conclusion to embark on one direction and not another can give rise to a 'period of consequences' in which the room for decision to manoeuvre is extremely restricted and in certain circumstances may be practically non-existent. Even in games, such as chess for example, situations can arise, brought on in part by one's own moves, in which the only move possible is that to which one is compelled. Hebbel expressed the position very well, as regards the innermost of human relations, in his tragedy *Herod and Mariamne:* 'The moment comes for every man, when the guide of his star hands him over the reins. The only bad thing is if he does not recognize the moment, and it is possible for anyone to miss it.'

Leaving aside this moment that is so important for the concrete conception of freedom, the objective existence of nodal points in the chain of decisions, analysis of this situation shows a further important determination in the specific character of the subject of the alternative—his inevitable ignorance of its consequences, or at least of some part of these. This structure pervades every alternative, at least to a certain extent; yet its quantitative aspect must also have qualitative reactions on the alternative itself. It is easy to see how everyday life, above all, poses perpetual alternatives which emerge unexpectedly and must often be responded to immediately at the risk of destruction. In these cases it pertains to the essential character of the alternative that its decision has to be made in ignorance of the majority of components of the situation and its consequences. But even here there is a minimum of freedom in the decision; here, too, there is still an alternative, even if as a marginal case, and not just a natural event determined by a purely spontaneous causality.

In a certain theoretically important sense, even the most rudimentary labour presents a kind of antithesis to the tendencies just described. If a 'period of consequences' can also occur in the labour process, this does not alter the basis of such an antithesis. For every positing in labour has its goal concretely and definitely fixed in thought; without this, no labour would be possible, whereas an alternative of the everyday type just described often has extremely confused and unclear goals. As always, of course, we assume here that labour is simply the creator of use-values. This means that the subject positing alternatives in the metabolism between man and nature is determined simply by his needs and his knowledge of the natural properties of his object; categories such as incapacity for certain types of labour as the result of the social structure (e.g., in slave labour), as well as alternatives of a social character that arise against the execution of labour (e.g., sabotage in highly developed social production) are not yet in existence at this level. Here, then, all that is relevant for successful realization is above all the adequate objective knowledge of the material and its processes; the so-called inner motive of the subject is scarcely at issue. The content of freedom is thus essentially distinct from that of the more complex forms. This could best be described by saying that the more adequate the knowledge of the relevant natural connections that the subject attains, the greater is his free movement in the material. Or to put it another way, the greater the adequate knowledge of the causal chains operative at the time, the most adequately can they be transformed into posited ones, and the more secure is the subject's mastery of them, i.e., the freedom that he attains here.

It is clear from all this that any decision between alternatives forms the centre of a social complex, with determinacy and freedom figuring among its components. The positing of a goal, which is how the ontologically new appears as social being, is an act of arising freedom, since the ways and means of the satisfaction of needs are no longer the results of spontaneously biological causal chains, but rather results of actions consciously decided on and executed. Simultaneously, however, and in a way inseparable from this, this act of freedom is determined directly by the need itself—mediated by those social relations that give rise to its type, quality, etc. This same duality, the simultaneous being and reciprocal relation between determinacy and freedom can also be established in the realization of the goal. All its means are originally given by nature, and this objectivity that it has determines all the acts of the labour process, which as we have seen, consists of a chain of alternatives. It is ultimately man who accomplishes the labour process, in his given facticity *[Geradesosein]* as the product of former development; no matter how much labour may alter him, even this process of change arises on the basis of the abilities that were present at the beginning of his labour, partly by nature, and partly socially formed already as co-determining moments, as possibilities in the sense of the Aristotelian *dynamis,* in the human performance of labour. Our earlier contention that every alternative is concrete in its ontological essence, and that a general alternative, an alternative as such is conceivable only as the mental product of a process of logical and epistemological abstraction, we can now make clearer in the sense that the freedom expressed in the alternative must necessarily be similarly concrete in its ontological nature, and not abstractly general. It presents a definite field of forces for decisions within a concrete social complex, in which both natural and social objectivities and forces come into play simultaneously with it. An ontological truth, therefore, can only pertain to this concrete totality. If in the course of development the social moments in the totality constantly increase, both absolutely and relatively, this cannot affect the basic given situation, all the less so in that in labour, as it is supposed here, the moment of mastery of nature must remain the decisive one, no matter how far-reaching the retreat of the natural boundary. Free movement in the material is and remains the predominant moment for freedom, in so far as this comes to prevail in the alternatives of labour.

But it should not be overlooked that the mode of appearance of freedom, both in form and in content, remains the same even when labour has already long since left behind the original condition that is taken here as the basis. We may refer above all to the rise of science (mathematics, geometry, etc.) from even stronger and more generalized experiences of labour. It is only natural that the immediate connection with the once concrete goal positing of the individual act of labour is loosened here. But an ultimate, even if possibly distantly mediated application in labour still remains as the ultimate verification, since even if in an extremely generalized manner, the ultimate intention of transforming real connections into posited ones, and such as are applicable in teleological positings, does not undergo any revolutionary change, so that neither does the mode of appearance of freedom that is characteristic of labour, free movement in the material, suffer any fundamental revolution. Even in the realm of artistic production, the condition is similar, although in this case the direct linkage with labour itself is relatively seldom transparent (the transformation of practices that are important to life, such as sowing, harvesting, hunting, warfare, etc., into dances; architecture). In this connection complications of various kinds arise, which we shall return to again later. Their basis lies on the one hand in that the immediate realization in labour itself is subjected here to very much diverse and often very heterogenous mediations, while on the other hand the material in which free movement in the material arises as the form of freedom is no longer simply nature, but rather in many cases already the metabolism between society and nature or even the process of social being itself. A really developed and comprehensive theory must naturally take these complications into consideration, and analyse them in detail, which again we shall only be able to do in our Ethics. It is sufficient for the moment simply to indicate these possibilities in connection with establishing that the basic form of freedom still remains the same here.

Since we have seen that an inseparable reciprocal relationship between determinacy and freedom obtains in this complex, it should not surprise us that the philosophical discussions of this question customarily proceed from the antithesis between necessity and freedom. Formulated in this way, the antithesis suffers firstly from the way that a philosophy generally oriented expressly towards logic and epistemology, and idealist philosophy in particular, simply identifies determination with necessity, something that implies a rationalistic generalization and overextension of the concept of necessity, an abstraction from its genuinely ontological 'if... then' character. Secondly, pre-Marxist philosophy, and idealist philosophy in particular, is dominated, as we have already seen, by an ontologically illegitimate extension of the concept of teleology to nature and history, by way of which it becomes extraordinarily difficult for it to grasp the problem of freedom in its proper and genuinely existing form. For this requires a correct grasp of the qualitative leap in the humanization of man, which is something radically new vis-à-vis the whole of nature, both organic and inorganic. Idealist philosophy, too, seeks to stress what is new here by the antithesis of necessity and freedom; but it reduces this newness not only by projecting into nature a teleology that is the ontological precondition of freedom, but also by using the ontological and structural antithesis. to dispense with nature and the categories of nature. We have for instance Hegel's celebrated and very influential definition of the relationship between freedom and necessity: 'Necessity is blind only so long as it is not understood.'[5]

Without a doubt, Hegel grasps here an essential aspect of the problem: the role of correct reflection, the correct grasp of the spontaneous causality that exists in itself. But even his term 'blind' already betrays the lopsidedness of the idealist conception which we have just been discussing. For this term only has a real meaning as an opposite to seeing; an object or process, etc., that can never be conscious or seeing, by virtue of its ontological nature, is not blind (or is so at most in an inexact and metaphorical sense); it falls short of any opposition between vision and blindness. What is ontologically correct in Hegel's dictum is that a causal process whose lawfulness (necessity) we have correctly grasped can lose for us that unmasterable character that Hegel seeks to describe by talking of blindness. Nothing, however, has changed in the natural causal process itself, it is simply that it can now be transformed into a process that is posited by us, and in this sense—but only in this—it ceases to operate as something 'blind'. The fact that what is involved here is not simply a pictorial expression—for in that case any polemical observation on it would be superfluous—is shown by the way that Engels himself speaks of the unfreedom of animals in dealing with this question: but a being can only be unfree if it has lost its freedom or has not yet attained it. Animals are not in fact unfree, they fall short of any opposition between free and unfree. But Hegel's definition of necessity contains something askew and erroneous even in a still more essential sense. This bears on his logical and teleological conception of the cosmos as a whole. Thus he summarizes his analysis of reciprocal action by saying that 'The truth of necessity, therefore, is freedom.'[6] We know from our critical presentation of Hegel's system and method that the definition of one category as the truth of another refers to the logical construction of the succession of categories, i.e., their place in the process by which substance is transformed into subject, on the path towards the identical subject-object.

By this abstractive rise into the metaphysical, both necessity and freedom, and so straightaway too their mutual relationship, lose that concrete sense that Hegel was seeking to give them, and which he had in many respects hit upon in his analysis of labour itself, as we already saw. This generalization sees the rise of a phantom identity, while proper necessity and freedom fall back to being improper representations of their concepts. Hegel summarizes their relationship as follows:

'Freedom and necessity, when thus abstractly opposed, are terms applicable only in the finite world to which, as such, they belong. A freedom involving no necessity, and mere necessity without freedom, are abstract and in this way untrue formulae of thought. Freedom is no blank indeterminateness: essentially concrete, and unvaryingly self-determinate, it is so far at the same time necessary. Necessity, again, in the ordinary acceptation of the term in popular philosophy, means determination from without only—as in finite mechanics, where a body moves only when it is struck by another body, and moves in the direction communicated to it by the impact. This however is a merely external necessity, not the real inward necessity which is identical with freedom.'[7]

Now we can really see how erroneous it was to describe necessity as 'blind'. Where the expression would have had a genuine meaning, Hegel sees 'a merely external necessity': yet this by its very nature cannot be transformed by becoming known, it remains 'blind', as we have seen, even when it is recognized in the labour process; only since it is recognized for the realization of a concrete teleological positing and transformed into a posited necessity, it fulfils its function in the given teleological context. (The wind is no less 'blind' than before if it helps to accomplish the posited movements of a windmill or a sailing ship.) The genuine necessity that Hegel describes as identical with freedom, however, remains a cosmic mystery.

Now if in his *Anti-Dühring* Engels refers back to Hegel's celebrated definition, he naturally dispenses with all constructions of this kind, without troubling to refute them. His conception is strictly and unambiguously oriented to labour.

'Freedom does not consist in the dream of independence from natural laws, but in the knowledge of these laws, and in the possibility this gives of systematically making them work towards definite ends. This holds good in relation both to the laws of external nature and to those which govern the bodily and mental existence of men themselves... Freedom of the will therefore means nothing but the capacity to make decisions with knowledge of the subject.'[8]

This is actually to turn Hegel's presentation 'onto its feet'; the only question is whether by still following Hegel's formulations and replacing the general concept of determination, which is somewhat vague at this level of generality, by the apparently more precise concept of necessity handed down by philosophical tradition, Engels has in fact really cleared up the ontological situation. We believe that the traditional counterposing of freedom and necessity cannot cope with the full scope of the problem at hand. Once we dispense with the logicizing exaggeration that is made of the concept of necessity, which played a major role not only in idealism and theology but also in the old materialist opposition to both of these, there is no basis for divorcing this completely from the other modal categories. Labour, and the teleologically posited process that constitutes it, is oriented towards reality; realization is not simply the real result that real men accomplish in struggle with reality itself in labour,

122

but also what is ontologically new in social being in opposition to the simple changing of objects in the processes of nature. Real man, in labour, confronts the entire reality that is involved in his labour, and in this connection we should recall that we never conceive reality as simply one of the modal categories, but rather as the ontological embodiment of their real totality. In this case, necessity (conceived as an 'if. . . then' connection, as the concrete lawfulness in question) is simply one component, if a most important one, of the complex of reality that is in question. Reality, however—conceived here as the reality of those materials, processes, circumstances, etc., that labour seeks to use for its positing of goals in the given case—is not completely exhausted by a long way in the connections, etc., defined by necessity.

We may refer in this connection to possibility. All labour presupposes that man recognizes the suitability of certain properties of an object for his positing of goals. These properties must certainly be objectively present, and belong to the being of the object in question, but in the natural being of the object they generally remain latent, as mere possibilities. (We recall that we have already indicated the ontological correlation of property and possibility above.) It is the objectively existent property of certain stones that when cut in a certain manner they can be used as a knife, an axe, etc. Without transforming this existent possibility of the natural into reality, however, all labour would be condemned to failure, would in fact be impossible. But no kind of necessity is recognized here, simply a latent possibility. It is not a blind necessity here that becomes a conscious one, but rather a latent possibility, which without the labour process will always remain latent, which is consciously raised by labour to the sphere of reality. But this is only one aspect of possibility in the labour process. The moment of transformation of the labouring subject that is stressed by all those who really understand labour, is, when considered ontologically, essentially a systematic awakening of possibilities that were previously dormant in man as mere possibilities. There are very probably few movements used in labour, e.g., ways of handling an object, etc., that were known or used at all before the labour process began. Only through labour were these raised from mere possibilities into capacities that enabled ever new possibilities in man to become realities, in a permanent process of development.

Finally, the role of chance, both positive and negative, should not be overlooked. The ontologically conditioned heterogeneity of natural being means that every activity is continuously affected by accidents. If the teleological positing is to be successfully realized, then man in his labour must also take continual account of these. This can be done in the negative sense, by his seeking to counter the possible consequences of unfavourable accidents and obviate the damage involved. But chance can also operate positively to raise the effectiveness of labour. Even at a far higher level of the scientific mastery of reality, cases are known in which accidents led to important discoveries. Even unfavourable chance situations may produce achievements that go beyond the point of departure. We may permit ourselves here to illustrate this by an apparently rather far-removed example. The walls on which Raphael painted his frescoes known as the Stanzas were pitted with a number of windows whose shape and form, etc., were extremely unfavourable for pictorial composition. The reason for this was quite fortuitous, since these rooms were there before the fresco project. But Raphael, in his Parnassus, and the Liberation of Peter, managed to exploit precisely this unfavourable accident to create extremely original and profoundly convincing and unique spatial forms. It seems obvious to us that similar problems arise time and again even in simple labour, particularly when, as with hunting, sailing, etc., this has to be performed in conditions that are very heterogenously determined. We believe, therefore, that the traditional definition of freedom as recognized necessity should be conceived as follows: Free movement in the material—speaking for the time being simply of labour—is only possible if the reality in question is correctly known in all its modal categorical forms, and correctly transformed in practice.

This extension of Engels's definition is not just unavoidable in the present case, if we want to get an adequate ontological grasp of the phenomenon of labour and its relationship to the freedom revealed in it; it equally indicates, for an important case, the methodology for completely superseding Hegelian idealism. Engels was certainly clearly and critically aware of the immediately visible idealist elements of Hegel's definition, and in a *de facto* materialist sense placed them 'on their feet'. Yet this critical reversal was only indirect. It escaped Engels that Hegel, as a consequence of his system, ascribed the category of necessity a logicistically exaggerated significance, and that he failed therefore to perceive the special and even categorically privileged specificity of reality itself, neglecting as a result to investigate the relationship of freedom to the total modality of reality. But since the only sure path from Hegel's dialectic to the materialist dialectic (and this was Marx's philosophical practice, and also Engels's in the majority of cases) consists in investigating every dialectical entwinement with respect to the ontological conditions underlying it, by way of an unconfined ontological criticism, the inadequacy of a simple 'materialist reversal' of Hegelian philosophy and idealism in general should be expressly indicated, when such an important, popular and influential passage is involved.

Apart from this methodological weakness, Engels recognized here clearly and precisely the specific kind of freedom arising in labour, what we have called 'free movement in the material'. He says that 'Freedom of the will therefore means nothing but the capacity to make decisions with knowledge of the subject.' At the time Engels was writing, this definition appeared completely sufficient for this level of freedom. The temporal conditions also explain why the problem we are dealing with here, the divergence at a possible higher level of development of the insights acquired through labour into either genuine, world-embracing science on the one hand, or mere technological manipulation on the other, escaped Engels here. As we have already shown, this parting of the ways is contained right from the beginning in the knowledge of nature that is aimed at in labour. It appeared, however, to have lost its relevance in the period between the Renaissance and the upsurge of scientific thought in the nineteenth century. This dual tendency was of course always implicitly present. Given the scanty general knowledge of early man as to the law-like character of natural processes, it was only too understandable that knowledge of nature should be deliberately focused and confined at first to the small island of the immediately knowable. Even when the development of labour led to the beginnings of the sciences, more extensive generalization had to be adapted to the ontological ideas of the time—magical, then later religious. This gave rise to an unavoidable apparent duality between the restricted rationality of labour itself, even if this was at times highly developed in its concrete context, and the extension and application of partial knowledge into a knowledge of the world and an orientation to those generalizations that are to be discovered in reality itself. It is sufficient to recall here how mathematical operations that were quite highly developed, relatively precise astronomic observations, were put in the service of astrology. This duality underwent its decisive crisis in the period of Copernicus, Kepler and Galileo. We have already mentioned how this period saw the appearance, in the person of Cardinal Bellarmini, of the theory of the deliberate, 'scientific' manipulation of science, its restriction, on principle, to a practicistic manipulation of the facts, laws, etc., that were recognized. It appeared for a long while—still at the time that Engels was writing—as if this attempt had been decisively doomed to failure; the advance of modern natural science, its generalization into a scientific world view, seemed to be irresistible.

It was only at the beginning of the twentieth century that the opposite tendency once more gained influence. And it is certainly no coincidence, as we have already shown, that the well-known positivist Duhem deliberately took up Bellarmini's conception and counterposed it to the position of Galileo, the position corresponding to the scientific spirit. The full unfurling of these tendencies in neopositivism has been depicted in detail in our first chapter, and so we need not return here to particular questions. From the standpoint of our present problem, we have the paradoxical situation that, whereas at a primitive level of development, the undeveloped character of labour and knowledge was an obstacle to genuine ontological investigation of being, today it is precisely the mastery of nature, limitlessly far-reaching in its extent, that sets up self-imposed barriers to a deepening and generalization of knowledge in an ontological sense, and that it is not against the fantasies of earlier days that this has to be directed, but rather against its own confinement on the basis of its own practical universality. The decisive themes in the antithesis between knowledge of being and its mere manipulation that appears here in a new form are something we can only treat in detail later on. Here we must be content to establish the fact that this manipulation has its material roots in the development of the productive forces, and its ideal roots in the new forms of the religious need, that it is no longer simply confined to the rejection of a real ontology, but actually opposes pure scientific development in practice. The American sociologist W. H. Whyte shows in his book *The Organization Man* that the new forms of organization of scientific research, planning, team work, etc., are by their very nature oriented towards technology, and that these forms already stand in the way of independent and scientifically productive research.[9] We mention only in passing that as far back as the 1920s Sinclair Lewis signalled this danger quite clearly in his novel *Martin Arrowsmith*. We have had to indicate the danger at this point, as its presence today makes extremely problematic Engels's definition of freedom at this level as 'the ·capacity to make decisions with knowledge of the subject'. For unlike magic, etc., manipulation in knowledge cannot be reproached with lack of knowledge of its subject. The problem is now centred on the goal to which this specialist knowledge is oriented; it is only this goal, and not just the specialist knowledge alone, that is able to furnish a real criterion, so that here too the criterion must be sought in the relationship to reality itself. Orientation to immediate practicality, no matter how solidly founded from a logical standpoint, leads into an ontological blind alley.

We have already pointed out earlier on that the original structure of labour undergoes certain essential changes once the teleological positing is no longer directed exclusively to the transformation of natural objects, the application of natural processes, but is also designed to cause other men to carry out positings of this kind in their turn. This change is still more qualitatively decisive when the course of development leads to man's own mode of behaviour, his own subjectivity, becoming the object of a teleological positing. The gradual, uneven and contradictory appearance of teleological positings of this kind is the result of social development. Thus the new forms can never be obtained from the original ones simply by intellectual derivation. Not only is their present concrete mode of appearance conditioned by society and history, but all their general forms, their very nature, is bound up with particular stages of development of social development. Before we have got to know their law-like characteristics, at least in their most general features, which we shall try to sketch in the next chapter in connection with the problem of reproduction, we can say nothing concrete about their mode of being, the connection and opposition of particular levels, the internal contradictoriness of individual complexes, etc. A proper treatment of these belongs in our Ethics. Here we can only attempt to indicate, and with the reservations already made, how, for all the complexities of structure, all qualitative antitheses in the object and hence in the end and means of the teleological positing, the decisive definitions still arise genetically from the labour process, and that while stressing the variation, which can even amount to opposition, this labour process can serve as a model for social practice even on the question of freedom.

The decisive variations arise by the object and medium of realization in the teleological positings becoming ever more social. This does not mean, as we know, that the natural basis disappears, simply that the exclusive orientation to nature that characterizes labour as we originally presupposed it is replaced by intentions that are objectively mixed in character, and become ever more strongly social. Even if nature is reduced to one aspect in these projects, the conduct towards it that became necessary in labour must still remain the same. But a second aspect now enters in. The social processes, conditions, etc., may well be resolved in the last analysis by human decisions between alternatives, but it should never be forgotten that these can only be socially relevant if they set in train causal series that move according to their own immanent laws, more or less independently of the intentions of their movers. Here, therefore, man as he acts in practice in society confronts a second nature, towards which, if he wants to master it successfully, he must directly behave to start with in the same way as towards the original nature, i.e., he must seek to transform the course of things that is independent of his consciousness into a posited course, to imprint on it, by knowledge of its nature, what he desires. Any rational social practice must take over at least this much from the original structure of labour.

This is already no small thing, but it is not all. For labour depends essentially on being, motion, etc., being completely indifferent, in nature, to our decisions; it is only the correct knowledge of nature that makes its practical mastery possible. Now social events may well have a similarly immanent and 'natural' lawfulness, and in this sense they take place just as independently of our alternatives as does nature itself. But if man intervenes in this course as an actor, an attitude towards the process is unavoidable, either affirmative or negative; whether this is conscious or unconscious, carried out with a true consciousness or a false, is something we cannot go into here; but this is not decisive for the kind of general treatment we are seeking to give at the moment. What we have in any case is a completely new moment in the complex of practice, and one which precisely influences the mode of being of the freedom that appears with it to a far-reaching extent. We have stressed in connection with labour how in its first form, as presupposed here, the inward subjective attitude has practically no role to play. Now, however, this becomes ever more important—of course in different ways in the different spheres in question. Freedom is not ultimately based on attitudes of this kind to the total process of society, or at least to its partial moments. Here, therefore, a new type of freedom arises on the basis of a labour gradually becoming social, a type that can no longer be derived directly from simple labour, and can no longer be reduced simply to free movement in the material. Yet some of its essential determinants still remain, as shown, even if with a varying weight in the different spheres of practice.

It goes without saying that the teleological positing and the alternative it involves must persist through all modifications, refinements and intensifications, as an essential aspect of any practice. The intimate and inseparable interplay of determinacy and freedom that characterizes this practice must also remain equally permanently. No matter how much the proportions may change, even bringing a qualitative change, the general basic structure cannot decisively alter. Perhaps the most significant change takes place in the relationship between end and means. We have seen how a certain relationship of potential contradiction existed between these already at the most primitive level, which however only begins to develop, both extensively and intensively, when it is a change in men, and no longer a change in nature, that comes to form the predominant moment. Of course, the inseparable coexistence of determination by the social reality and freedom in the alternative decision, remains in existence throughout. But there is still a qualitative difference as to whether the content of the alternative is simply something that can be determined as correct or incorrect by knowledge alone, or whether the posited goal itself is the result of alternatives posed by man and society. For it is clear enough that once class societies have arisen, any question leads to different solutions according to the standpoint from which the answer to an actual dilemma is sought. And it is equally evident that as the social character of society becomes ever stronger, these alternatives in the foundations of the alternative projects must constantly increase in both breadth and depth. It is not yet possible here to analyse these changes in the structure of posited goals in any concrete manner. But by simply expressing the fact that such a direction of development must occur here, we show that the positing of goals can no longer be measured by the same criteria as simple labour.

This situation has the necessary result that the contradictions between the positing of the goal and the means of its realization must accordingly grow sharper, until they become qualitatively decisive. Even here, of course, the question as to whether the means are suitable for realizing the posited goal will stand in the foreground. But firstly, so great a distinction arises in the possibility of exactly deciding this question, that it must immediately appear as a qualitative one. For in the positing of causal chains in simple labour, what is involved is the knowledge of effective natural causalities that are inherently unchanged. The question is simply how far their enduring nature and naturally conditioned variations are correctly recognized. But now the 'material' of the causal positings to be achieved in the means is of a social character, i.e., possible human decisions between alternatives; hence something that is on principle not homogeneous, and also in constant change. This would naturally mean such a level of uncertainty in the causal positing that it would be quite correct to speak of a qualitative difference from original labour. And this qualitative difference is actually present, though decisions are known to us from history by which this uncertainty in knowledge of the means has been successfully overcome. On the other hand, we see time and again that the modern attempts to master this uncertainty with methods of manipulation prove extremely problematic in the more complicated cases.

A question that seems still more important from our standpoint is that of the possible contradiction between the positing of the goal and the prolonged action of the means. Here there arises an important social problem of the kind that very soon experienced a general philosophical treatment, and, one could say, has permanently remained on the agenda of thought. Both empiricists in social practice and their moralistic critics find themselves compelled here to struggle with this contradiction time and again. Without going into concrete questions of detail here, which again will be possible only in the Ethics, we must at least stress once more the theoretical superiority of the ontological treatment of social practice, both vis-à-vis practicistic empiricism and vis-à-vis abstract moralism. History often shows, on the one hand, how means that appeared from a rational standpoint adequately adapted to certain posited goals 'suddenly' misfire completely and catastrophically, and on the other hand, how it is impossible—even from the standpoint of a genuine ethics—to draw up *a priori* a rationalized table of permissible and impermissible means. It is only possible to refute both these false extremes from a standpoint from which men's moral, ethical, etc., motivations appear as real moments of social being, which always become more or less effective within social complexes that are contradictory, but unitary even in their contradictions, and which always form real components of social practice, playing a decisive role in it because of this property of theirs as to whether a certain means (a certain influencing of men to decide their alternatives this way or that) is suitable or unsuitable, correct or reprehensible, for the realization of a goal.

So that a preliminary definition of this kind (and one that is thus necessarily very abstract) should not lead to misunderstandings, we must add something that already necessarily follows from our former discussions: that the ontological reality of ethical, etc., behaviour in no way means that recognition of this reality can exhaust its nature. On the contrary. Its social reality depends not least on the values arising from social development with which it is actually linked, how it is really linked with their persistence, decline, etc. If this aspect were to be made absolute, in an impermissible way, then we would arrive at an idealist conception of the socio-historical process; if it were simply negated, one would arrive at the kind of irrationality that indelibly marks all forms of practicistic *'Realpolitik'*, even those that appeal verbally to Marx. One must therefore take care, even in this necessarily very abstract and general treatment, to insist that the growing importance of subjective decisions in the alternatives that is revealed here is first and foremost a social phenomenon. It is not that the objectivity of the developmental process becomes subjectively relativized—this is simply a socially conditioned form of appearance of its immediacy—but rather the objective process itself that raises tasks, as a function of its higher development, which can only be undertaken as a result of this growing importance of subjective decisions. But all value judgements that acquire their validity in these subjective decisions are anchored in the social objectivity of values, in their importance for the objective development of the human species, and both their positive or negative value and the intensity and persistence of their effect are ultimately the products of this objective social process.

It is not difficult to see how far removed the structures of behaviour that thus arise are from those of simple labour. Nevertheless, it will be clear to any unprejudiced view that, considered ontologically, the kernels, if only the kernels, of these conflicts and contradictions are already contained in the most simple end-means relationship. If the social and historical actualization of this relationship gives rise to complexes of problems that are completely novel even in quality, this can only surprise those who do not conceive history as the ontological reality of social being and hence either hypostatize values into 'timeless' entities of pure spirit, or else see in them merely subjective reflexes to objective processes that cannot be influenced by human practice.

The situation is very similar with the effects produced by labour in its full compass. Here too, the distinctions are necessarily very important; yet the most important aspect of the nature of this process persists amid the greatest concrete changes. What we have in mind here are those effects that labour brings about in the working man himself: the necessity for his self-control, his constant battle against his own instincts, emotions, etc. We have already noted, but must repeat it here with special emphasis, that it is precisely in this struggle, this struggle against his own naturally given properties, that man has come to be man, and that his further development and perfection can only be accomplished by the same path and with these same means. It is no accident that even the customs of primitive peoples place this problem at the centre of properly human behaviour; nor that every great moral philosophy, from Socrates, the Stoics and Epicurus through to such different thinkers as Spinoza and Kant, had permanently wrestled with this problem as the central question of truly human behaviour. In labour itself, of course, what is involved is simply a question of suitable means: It can only be successful, can only produce use-values, useful things, if this self-control of the subject is a permanent feature of the labour process; this is the case also with any other practical goal that is posited. But this could still be considered by itself as merely a formal similarity in practice.

What is involved, however, already in labour itself, is something much more. Irrespective of how far the performer of this labour is aware of it, in this process he produces himself as a member of the human race, and hence produces the human race itself. We may even say that the path of struggle for self-mastery, from natural determination by instinct to conscious self-control, is the only real path to true human freedom. The proportions in which human decisions are based in nature and in society may be contested, and the aspect of determinacy in any particular positing of a goal, any decision between alternatives, may be assessed as high as you like; but the struggle for control over oneself, over one's own originally purely organic nature, is quite certainly an act of freedom, a foundation of freedom for human life. Here we encounter the problem of the species character in human being and freedom: the overcoming of the mere organic muteness of the species, its forward development into the articulated and self-developing species of man who forms himself into a social being, is from the ontological and genetic standpoint the same act as that of the rise of freedom.

The existentialists try to rescue freedom intellectually, and to elevate it, when they speak of man's being 'thrown' into freedom, of man being 'condemned'* to freedom. In reality, however, any freedom that is not rooted in man's social being, that does not develop from this, even if by a leap, is a phantom. If man had not made himself into a social species-being in and by labour, if freedom were not the fruit of his own activity, of his overcoming his own merely organic character, then there could be no real freedom at all. If the freedom won in the original labour was necessarily still rudimentary and restricted, this in no way alters the fact that the most spiritual and highest freedom must be fought for with the same methods as in the original labour, and that its outcome, even if at a much higher stage of consciousness, has ultimately the same content: the mastery of the individual acting in the nature of his species over his merely natural and particular individuality. In this sense, we believe, labour really can be taken as a model for all freedom.

It was with these considerations that we started our discussion of labour, in the sense presupposed, even earlier on, in connection with the higher forms of appearance of human practice. This we had to do, for while labour in this sense, as simply the producer of use-values, is certainly the genetic beginning of man's humanization, each of its aspects contain real tendencies that necessarily lead far beyond this original condition. But even though this original condition of labour is a historical reality, whose constitution and extension took a seemingly endless period of time, we were correct to call our assumption an abstraction, a rational abstraction in the sense used by Marx. This meant that we deliberately omitted, time and again, the necessary social environment which develops together with labour, so as to elaborate the characteristics of labour itself in the purest form possible. This was of course not possible without pointing out time and again the affinities and antitheses between labour and the higher social complexes.

I believe we have now reached the point at which this abstraction can and must be definitively brought to an end, so that we can embark on the analysis of the underlying dynamic of society, its reproduction process. This will form the content of the next chapter.

NOTES

(Introduction)
1   Marx, *Capital* Volume 1, Harmondsworth, 1976, p. 133.

Section 1: Labour as a Teleological Positing
1   Engels, 'The Role of Labour in the Transition from Ape to Man', in *Dialectics of Nature,* Moscow, 1972, p. 171.
2   *Capital* Volume 1, pp. 283-4.
3   N. Hartmann, *Teleologisches Denken,* Berlin, 1951, p. 13.
4   Kant, *Critique of Judgement,* § 75.
5   Engels to Marx, c. 12 December 1859, and Marx to Engels, 19 December 1860.
6   *Critique of Judgement,* § 77.
7   Aristotle, *Metaphysics,* Book Z, Chapter VII (trans. Warrington, London, 1956, pp. 181 ff).
8   *Teleologisches Denken,* pp. 68 ff.
9   Hegel, *Jenenser Realphilosophie,* Leipzig, 1932, II, pp. 198 ff. [quoted in Lukács, *The Young Hegel,* Merlin Press, 1975, pp. 344-5.]
*   *Gebietskategorie*—the manuscript could possibly be also read as *Gebürtskategorie,* 'category of birth'.
10 Hegel, *Science of Logic,* transl. Miller, London, 1969, p. 747.
*   (p. 17). Here the manuscript contains the addition 'in many cases'.
11 Gordon Childe, *Man Makes Himself,* London, 1966, p. 93.
12 J.D. Bernal, *Science in History,* Harmondsworth, 1969, p. 124.
13 Marx and Engels, *Collected Works,* vol. 5, p. 3.
14 A. Gehlen, *Der Mensch,* Bonn, 1950, pp. 43 and 67.
15 Aristotle, *Metaphysics,* Book Δ, Chapter XII.
16 ibid., Book θ, Chapter VIII, pp. 237-9.
*   (p. 35). The manuscript adds: 'apparatus'.
17 *Grundrisse,* Harmondsworth, 1973, p. 300.
*   (p. 38). The manuscript adds: 'in advance'.
18 *Capital* Volume 1, p. 283.

Section 2: Labour as a Model for Social Practice
1   *Collected Works,* Vol. 5, p. 3.
2   *Collected Works,* Vol. 1, p. 104.
3   P. Duhem, *Essai sur la nature de la théorie physique de Platon à Galilée,* Paris, 1908, pp. 77 ff. and 128 ff.
4   H. Poincaré, *Science and Hypothesis,* (German edn., 1960, p. 118).
*   (p. 64). The manuscript adds: 'purely'.
5   Kant, *Fundamental Principles of the Metaphysics of Ethics,* transl. Abbott, London, 1965, p. 53.
6   Kant, *Critique of Practical Reason* (German edn., 1906, pp. 24 ff.)
7   Lukács, *The Young Hegel,* Merlin Press, 1975, pp. 293 ff.

8 Hegel, *Philosophy of Right* (transl. Knox), Oxford, 1973, pp. 76 (§ 108) and 248 (Addition).
9 Hegel, *Philosophy of Mind* (transl. Wallace and Miller), Oxford, 1971, § 482; pp. 231-2.
10 *Capital*, Volume 1, p. 177.
11 ibid., p. 131.
12 St Augustine, *Confessions*, London, 1960, Vol. I, pp. 375-7 (Book VII, Chapters 11-12).
13 Hobbes, *Leviathan* (ed. Plamenatz), London, 1962, p. 90.
14 Spinoza, *Ethics* (transl. Elwes), New York, 1955, Part IV, Preface p. 189.
15 See *Collected Works*, Vol. 5, pp. 409 ff.
16 Hegel, *Lectures on the History of Philosophy*, Vol. II, London, 1894, p. 261.
17 *Capital*, Volume 1, pp. 201, 208-9.
18 *Grundrisse*, p. 173.
19 ibid., p. 711.
20 ibid., p. 712.
* (p. 90). The following footnote occurs at this point in the manuscript: 'We recall our discussions of this question in the chapter on Marx, particularly Marx's letter to Lassalle, etc.'
* (p. 92). *Pharsalia* 1, 128. 'The victorious cause pleased the gods, but the defeated cause pleased Cato.'

Section 3: The Subject-Object Relationship in Labour and its Consequences
1 *Dialectics of Nature*, p. 173. ('The Role of Labour in the Transition from Ape to Man').
2 ibid., pp. 177-8.
3 E. Ch. Welskopf, *Probleme der Musse im alten Hellas*, Berlin, 1962, p. 47.
4 Max Weber, *The Sociology of Religion* (from *Economy and Society*), London, 1966, p. 85.
5 *Hegel's Logic* (transl. Wallace), Oxford, 1975, § 147, Addition; p. 209.
6 ibid., § 158; p. 220.
7 ibid., § 35, Addition; pp. 55-6.
8 *Anti-Dühring*, London, 1969, pp. 136-7.
9 W.H. Whyte, *The Organization Man*, Harmondsworth, 1960, pp. 190 ff.
* The manuscript adds 'Être et néant'.

Georg Lukács: TOWARD THE ONTOLOGY OF SOCIAL
BEING

General Contents
(Part Two, Chapter 1, which forms the contents of the
present volume, is printed in italics.)

Printed in the United States
107170LV00005B/8/A

9 780850 362558